VOLLEYBALL

FOR COACHES AND TEACHERS

Second Edition

Frances Schaafsma
Ann Heck
Connie Throneberry Sarver

VOLLEYBALL

FOR COACHES AND TEACHERS

Contents

Preface

This book is designed to have application for coaches and teachers at all skill levels and is organized so that the material that has application for a specific level of play can easily be identified and extracted for use.

The main purpose of this book is to assist the teacher and the coach in gaining insights into procedures that will effectively assist girls and women to learn and enjoy volleyball at all levels of skill. More specifically, an attempt has been made to (1) summarize and evaluate current performance practices in volleyball and suggest alternative approaches to teaching and coaching for all skill levels; (2) provide suggestions for conducting a competitive program for volleyball and to explore some of the circumstances that are attendant to the competitive situation in volleyball; and (3) stimulate the teacher and the coach to be an analyst and student of the game who chooses methods of performance for considered reasons rather than to be an imitator of all the latest fads without cause.

The majority of the material presented focuses upon the rudiments of volleyball including individual technical and team tactical skills. Fundamental and advanced skills are analyzed mechanically with the aid of visuals. Special considerations are given to identifying the performance errors that the teacher will see at various stages of the learning process. Suggestions are made with regard to progressions and instructional cues that should help the player avoid errors or correct them.

An attempt has been made to analyze volleyball performances as executed by skilled women players so that reasonable expectations for girls and women are identified. The problems that are usually encountered by the female player are categorized, and ideas are presented to aid the teacher or coach in developing progressions for practice to speed up the mastery of techniques and the understanding of the game.

Rationale is given for all methods of performance and tactics recommended. Whenever possible, alternative methods are explored with a discussion of the factors that would influence the choice of one method over another.

Strategies in common use for offense and defense are thoroughly presented. The problems in choice of offensive and defensive systems are discussed. Special attention is given to decisions regarding systems of play and their applicability at various skill levels.

Practice situations and drills for skill have been categorized according to purpose and demands for skill. These have been placed at the end of each chapter to facilitate their use by the teacher and coach.

A brief discussion of motor learning principles and teaching methodology is presented with specific reference to application in teaching volleyball. These principles are extended for use by the coach for the competitive situation. Special sections of the book are devoted to the considerations necessary in conducting the competitive program in volleyball. These may, however, be useful for the teacher as well, including aspects of warm-up, conditioning, evaluation of performance, and game situation alternatives.

A bibliography is presented at the end of chapters whenever appropriate. Selected references that span the several chapters on techniques and strategies are given at the end of the book.

Introduction

Since its inception in 1895, the sport of volleyball has undergone tremendous change and growth. It has evolved from a game which was conceived as a recreational and competitive activity, requiring limited skill and conditioning, to a game demanding highly refined strategies, techniques, speed, agility, power and endurance.

The major impetus for the changes which have occurred was the inclusion of volleyball in the Olympic Games in Tokyo in 1964. The Olympic competition demonstrated to Americans the developments that had occurred in volleyball techniques and strategies in the European and Asian countries. Play in the Olympic Games and World Games in subsequent years has generated interest in volleyball in the United States as an exciting athletic game for both males and females of all ages.

The fascination of American girls and women for this style of aggressive and power play has been phenomenal. Throughout the United States, workships, camps, clinics and institutes have been conducted to aid teachers and coaches in becoming more knowledgable and skillful in teaching and coaching. Books such as VOLLEYBALL FOR COACHES AND TEACHERS, have helped in the effort to promote the sport and aid instructors and participants to have a comprehensive and accurate analysis of the technical and tactical aspects of the game. These combined efforts have made significant contributions in the improvement of teaching and coaching, and have resulted in improved skill development and higher level competition.

Acknowledgments

Sincere appreciation is expressed to the players who contributed their time and skill in demonstrating the various playing techniques and team strategies: Jennie de Coup-Crank, Kathryn DeBolt, Maureen Flory, Lydia Goodshall, Rhonda Hoenisch, Jan Kenyon, Sharon Modglin, Vicki Morris, Heidi Smith, and Wendy Wellsfry.

A special thank you is expressed to Sheila Reed for her dedicated efforts in creating the drawings, and to Steven Hurlbert for the excellent quality of photography characteristic of all the photographed figures.

Part One

Motor Learning and Skilled Performance

1

Motor Learning and Skilled Performance

The volleyball coach is anxious to have players enter competition with self-confidence and keen desire to do their best. This attitude is developed only if players have learned the techniques and strategy that will be required in the match and know exactly what is expected of them. The players should know that they are equal to whatever may occur. This comes only through learning and practice.

One of the constant functions of the coach is that of teaching. Teaching is filled with decision-making circumstances, and among the teaching-oriented questions a coach must often deal with are: What techniques must be mastered for effective team play? Are players performing the basic techniques effectively or are changes necessary? If changes are needed, what is the best method? When is a player ready to progress to more difficult techniques? How long will it take to learn a new tactic so it can be performed in the game?

When will I know that a player has learned a technique? Why do some players learn more quickly than others? How much can a player be expected to remember from practice to game?

To be a good teacher and to be able to deal with questions similar to those above, the coach must possess some knowledge of the learning process and what factors or conditions speed up or retard the process.

In recent years much research has been done to find out more about human performance and motor skill learning. The bibliography for this chapter contains a representation of the published material which might serve the teacher or coach who is interested in pursuing study in this area.

The following sections present a simplified overview of learning and some of the factors affecting it with illustrations drawn for application in coaching volleyball.

Skill

While watching a volleyball match it is easy to distinguish the skilled from the unskilled player. The skilled player is effective in carrying out her intent—she "gets the job done." She is consistent and efficient in her efforts, that is, she makes few errors and wastes little effort in unimportant movements. Her reactions to the game situation are almost automatic; she appears to execute techniques without thinking about how to do them, yet makes minute performance variations as the situation demands. She is aware of teammates, opponents and the ball at all times, monitoring the situation for cues which would indicate the appropriate strategy to use. The unskilled player, on the other hand, demonstrates few, if any, of the above qualities. She is often unable to pass or set the ball as she intends, though she works very hard to accomplish the task. She is often a step too slow in reaction for the play, and often chooses the wrong technique or tactic for a given situation.

Skilled performance in volleyball, as in any other sport, does not just happen. It is the result of learning the movements and tactics of the game to a point where responses are automatic and not negatively affected by emotion level or changes in the game circumstances such as a crowd or an unorthodox play by the opponent. It is the function of the coach to assist the player to develop skill. This can be a challenging and exciting experience for both.

Form

"Good form" is the method of performing a given technique which is considered to be the best method. This best method attempts to capitalize on the proper use of mechanical principles such as leverage, balance, and force production for efficiency and effectiveness. What is accepted as "good form" changes from time to time as players and coaches experiment and find better ways of performing. For instance, there is some discussion over the footwork for the approach to the spike. Basically, two methods are used. One is done with a stride/stride/step-close while the other is done with a stride to a two-foot jump. In both cases, the player leaves the court from two feet with a vigorous arm swing upward. One approach may be more suited to the natural jumping rhythm of the player than the other, and should be considered by the coach and player in determining the most effective technique.

Most coaches would teach "good form" to a beginner or a player learning a new technique. Although form should be taught, style should be allowed to develop in an individual way as skill develops. Style reflects the individual player's mannerism in doing a given technique. Style factors may be the result of personality, body build or other individual characteristics. The manner in which a player tilts the head or finishes a movement with a flourish is an example of style.

Often the coach is confronted with the decision whether to change the form of a player who uses unorthodox technique. An example is the spiker who has transferred the basketball lay-up approach to the spike, taking off with one foot. The use of the unorthodox technique may limit the extent of the player's eventual improvement. Restructuring the technique takes time. These factors should be weighed and the decision reached by consultation between player and coach. The player must realize that she may be momentarily frustrated by a deterioration of performance and that she must work very hard in practice to make the change. If it seems worth it to her, the change can be made.

More often, however, the coach will be called on to assist players make minor adaptations in their form which will make performance more effective. The setter who needs more leg thrust to push sets wide to the sideline may need to work on bending the knees a little more deeply prior to the set to get the desired leg action. A player may need to alter the position of the serve toss slightly to assure greater accuracy. These changes occur more quickly than the one mentioned above, but do require practice to accomplish.

Learning

Learning has taken place when a player has been able to change her performance of a technique so that she can execute the change at will, and does not revert back to earlier tendencies at a later time. For learning to occur practice must take place. A player may vary in performance from time to time due to physical, psychological, or environmental factors such as fatigue, ill health, boredom, or distractions. To get a fair measure of the amount of learning that has taken place a player must be observed under ideal performance conditions. A spiker who has been making good progress in practice might not be able to keep the ball in court during her first real match of the season. This does not necessarily mean that she has not been learning the spike. It does mean that she will have to practice more to move her performance further along on the continuum of skill to be able to consistently spike with accuracy. She may also need more experience to learn to deal with the emotional overtones of a real match.

The learning process for motor skill development is a complex one but can be divided into some specific phases. The first phase is motivation—the player must want to learn and be interested in continuing to work once the learning process has started. Secondly, the player must understand what it is she is to do—she must develop a concept of the technique or strategy. Next, she must practice, and as practice occurs she will make adaptations in performance that will bring her execution of the technique more and more in line with what she perceives the ideal to be. Finally, as the player gains in experience and practice of the technique, she will become better able to do it automatically, thus being free to concentrate on game strategy.

When an ineffective technique has already been learned, the process of restructuring a new performance pattern is somewhat different. Motivation to do it is necessary. The player must then be helped to identify the parts of the pattern to be changed and know how to change them. This is followed by practice on the parts to be changed, and then practice on the whole technique with conscious effort to make the specific changes until the new pattern is automatic.

The following sections will summarize some elements that are present when considering the phases of the learning process, as described above.

To learn the forearm pass properly the player must want to do so. There are *Motivation* many reasons why a woman might want to play volleyball and learn the forearm pass. She may be interested and curious after watching someone else do it. She may have a personal need, such as wanting to be successful in something, wanting to be accepted into the group that is playing volleyball, wanting to emulate someone she admires, or wanting to gain the approval of someone she admires. Many girls are attracted to volleyball participation for the co-ed opportunities it affords and will work very hard to develop skill in the co-ed situation. Others wish to participate in a vigorous competitive sport and find that this is a place in the American culture where it is socially acceptable for a woman to develop skill and demonstrate a good deal of aggressiveness, strength, and power.

There are also a number of negative reasons to cause women to work hard to develop skill. These include a fear of failure, fear of punishment, or the threat of status in a group. For instance, there are a few coaches on the international level who are known to threaten and deliver physical punishment to players who do not perform up to expectation, since failure will reflect upon the country one represents. This tactic has resulted, in some cases, in a very high level of skill. It is doubtful, however, if the fear, frustration, and anguish experienced by the player are worth the end result.

Most people who participate in sport do so for the joy and the exhilaration derived from the movement and a satisfying performance. To insure that players have the opportunity to experience the enjoyment that volleyball affords, the coach should stimulate action through the positive and avoid the negative methods.

To change performance of an ineffective technique it is also necessary for a player to want to make the change. Some players will be resistant to change. This may be a result of a fear of failure, lack of confidence in the coach, loyalty to a prior coach or instructor who advocated that method of performance, or not being convinced a change is necessary. These barriers must be bridged before any progress can be made.

Once the player has begun to learn the forearm pass, it is necessary for her to maintain interest and concentration so that progress can be made. The first requirement is that she must know what she is to do. At first this may be simply to try to copy the coach's demonstration. Then, for the forearm pass, it may progress to being able to pass the ball straight ahead at a given height. The player may then be challenged to move to her right and left to receive the ball for the pass, and then to receive balls traveling at various speeds. This procedure, or progressively increasing the expectations, continues until the player is able to use the forearm pass in game situations.

It is noted that the first step in maintaining interest is to establish a specific goal. The goal should be one that is reasonable for the player, one that can be reached with some effort. With repeated success, the goal is raised. With repeated failure the goal is simplified. The role of the coach is to assist the player in deciding the goals which might be reached and to help her to plot the method of reaching the goals through sound technique.

As the goals are set and periodically raised another factor is necessary to maintain interest. The player should know how she is doing in relation to the goal which was established; she should receive feedback. The simplest means of accomplishing this is for the coach to comment with reference to the quality of the performance. Of course, the player will usually get some instant feedback by being able to see the flight of the ball as she completes a forearm pass. If the pass is the proper height and position she may know that she has had some success. At beginning levels, however, the player may not have a clear concept of what constitutes "proper" flight and so a comment like "nice pass" or "a little higher" may be needed. Other methods which may give the player information about her performance include video-taping or filming it and evaluating in relation to the ideal of performance. Statistics, incidence charts, and rating scales may also be useful in helping a player to know how she is progressing. Regardless of the methods used, to be effective, feedback should be as immediate as possible.

Concept Development Before learning to spike the ball the player must have a concept of correct technique. The best method of gaining the concept is by watching a skilled player spike the ball. Whether this is a live or filmed demonstration is of little consequence. The important factors are that the demonstration should be as accurate as possible and done in the same timing expected in performance. Two or more repetitions are necessary to gain the concept. Live simulation of slow motion is not desirable since it distorts the action and timing factors of the real performance. Slow motion filmed demonstration may be useful, but should be preceded and followed by up-to-speed repetitions of the technique to reestablish the concept of time.

The beginner will not be able to see all the details of the spike at first, so a general verbal description to guide the viewing may be helpful. The viewer may be directed to note the starting position, the fact that the player jumps to hit the ball, and that the ball is hit downward over the net. Usually the viewer will follow the flight of the ball and will not see the follow-through. Detailed verbal description will have very little meaning for the player until later when she has had a chance to try the spike. Attention should be given to providing a good angle for viewing, and distractions, such as too much narration, nervous mannerisms of the demonstrator, or loose balls rolling about the court should be avoided.

By trying the spike the player will gain a better idea about what to do. But since a spike is a rather complex technique, it may be necessary to break it down so that the player may gain a concept of the approach and jump separate from the contact and follow-through. After each part is tried the whole spike is attempted. This whole-part-whole method is effective for gaining the concept of the spike, whereas the less complex techniques of the overhand and forearm passes may be approached as wholes.

With initial trials of the spike the player may try to relate it to previous experiences which are similar, such as the softball throw, the tennis serve, or the badminton overhead smash. If the technique chosen for relationship was learned in a manner consistent with that desired in the spike it may facilitate the learning of the spike. If the tennis serve or the overhead throw was learned with an arm and shoulder movement which is slightly different from the one desired in the spike progress in learning the spike correctly may be impeded. For example, many fine young women athletes learn to throw a softball with a slight sidearm motion, releasing the ball with an outward rotation of the wrist, or supination. This can interfere with the learning of the spike since proper execution of the spike requires the player to fully extend the arm upward and to hit the ball with the hand squarely behind it and with the wrist snapping forward, or flexing with slight pronation. The coach must be aware of the performance requirement for each technique in volleyball so that the player may be given help at this stage in constructing the appropriate concept.

After a number of trials the player will be able to make sense out of more detailed verbal directions. She might also benefit from seeing the spike demonstrated again. At this time, as well, the coach can begin to structure key cues with the player which may be of use in later coaching. For instance, the approach to the spike is usually not begun until the set is off the setter's hands so that the spiker can make adjustment to the position of the ball. Often the beginner will start the approach too soon. The cue "wait for the set" or "wait," if understood in context, will have meaning for the player and elicit a complete concept to her when she hears it. There are numerous key words or cues which can be associated with the performance for each technique and strategy of volleyball. If these are structured with the concept of what is to be done the coach can have direct and simple communication with the player. The coach must be certain, however, that the player has a clear understanding of the cue. Often the reason a player does not respond to coaching cues is that she does not have a clear understanding of the cue to guide her action.

In addition to establishing cues for coaching, it may be helpful to explain the fundamental mechanical principles which are basic to executing the technique. For example, in the spike, an approach is taken to aid in getting height in the jump. An understanding of the principles of maintaining momentum and converting forward momentum into upward momentum may be useful to the player in becoming more aware of the demands of the technique and more self-directing in developing skill.

In some instances players may be unable to kinesthetically perceive their own actions when they try to spike, and so need help in feeling what the correct positioning should be. It may be helpful to physically move the player through the desired pattern. This works effectively in helping the sidearm thrower to feel the extent to which the elbow must be raised in the spike. Other players may have difficulty patterning the sequence of the spike movement. It is beneficial for the player to mimetically follow the pattern of a skilled player or the coach. This is especially true in learning the footwork and jump sequence. Usually a number of repetitions are necessary to get the feel of the pattern and the timing.

Practice and Adaptation

Practice begins with the first trial the player makes after gaining the idea about what to do. Mere repetition of the techniques does not insure that skill will increase. Practice must proceed with specific objectives in the mind of the player. While practicing the overhand pass the player should concentrate on correct positioning of the feet and on proper use of the body to develop force. Eventually she should work on accurate trajectory and placement of the ball, and then should practice moving to the ball with good footwork.

Before these objectives of performing the pass can become this specific, however, the player will have made a number of adaptations since the first trial. If she has gotten the concept of the technique her first attempts will look a good deal like the proposed technique, but she will have success only at random. She will begin to try to figure out what caused the success and try to repeat the things that made it happen. Her strategy in executing the technique will vary from trial to trial as she experiments.

So that learning does not proceed simply by trial and error, the coach can speed up the process by making comments to the player to direct her efforts. Cues for performance can be introduced gradually as the player is able to understand them. The cues used should be positive. It is more helpful to tell a player to contact the bottom of the ball in the overhand pass than to tell her that she is passing the ball in a trajectory that is too low. Of course, it means that the player may need help in selecting the best way to successfully contact the bottom of the ball.

This stage of the learning process can either be extremely exciting or terribly frustrating to the player. The expectations for progress should be reasonable and the player should know how well she is doing. When a player is making progress the coach may be overanxious to accelerate the progress. In so doing, the coach will often dwell on error correction which will give the player the feeling that she can do nothing right, when in reality she is making rapid progress. It is important to point out the success and allow the player time to feel the satisfaction that it involves. This is important to the development of self-confidence and a feeling of well-being which are so necessary to the total enjoyment of skilled performance.

Another form of practice is mental practice. This is done by spending some time conceptualizing the correct performance and thinking about going through the motions without actually moving. This may enhance performance to a degree when combined with actual practice.

When the player has learned to perform the fundamental essentials of a technique, she should gain experience in using the technique in the various situations which will occur in the match. The overhead pass should be practiced as a front set, a back set, a backcourt set and a cross-court set. To expect a player to perform well in the pressure of competition it is important for her to have had practice experience in all the potential game situations. She must be aware of the choices of technique and strategy that each game situation presents and have practice in masking and performing the choices. Practice progression and drills for developing technique into game responses are given at the end of each chapter on techniques.

At early stages of learning practice time spent on each specific aspect of skill development should be kept very short. As skill increases the player will be able to concentrate on specific objectives for longer periods of time and may be highly motivated to work for extended periods of time. A limiting factor on the length of the practice time is fatigue. A high level of conditioning will delay the onset of fatigue. However, it is doubtful that practice after the onset of excessive fatigue is beneficial. Fatigue may cause a player to make errors and, therefore, practice errors. Also, as fatigue develops the vulnerability for injury increases.

Team practice periods should be a reasonable length of time. The session should be planned so that the activity has variety. An extended session on the serve would become very boring after a time. Work on the serve interspersed with work on a more active aspect of the game would maintain interest. The items to be worked on in practice should vary in the demands placed on the player, both in terms of the parts of the body used and the amount of concentration and exertion required. Players should know the purpose of each phase of practice. They should be encouraged to begin to evaluate their own performance needs and work to find ways of meeting these needs. A player who repeatedly falls into the net on the follow-through of the spike knows she has a problem. The coach can help her to understand and correct the error, but it is up to the player to concentrate her efforts during practice to make the change.

The ideal at this stage of learning and performance is that the player begin to know what to do and how to do it. She should begin to feel her own actions and analyze her results so that she can make the adaptations necessary in the game situation. The ultimate aim is to free the player from the direction of the coach in the performance of the specific techniques and tactics of the game.

The Automatic Action

At highest levels of skill the player is able to perform all the techniques of the game with consistency. This frees her to concentrate on tactics and strategy. To reach this level overlearning must occur. It means that the player must serve, pass, set, spike, and block the ball so many times and in the various ways these techniques are used, that in the game each response will be automatic.

Even when the stage of automatic action has been achieved a player is subject to lapses of timing or reaction. When this happens during competition the coach may be able to offer a key cue word which will direct the player back toward the right course of action. If this fails it will be counter productive to analyze the problems with the player during the competition. This will usually lead to further deterioration of performance. It may be beneficial to rest the player for a brief period. Often after a period of no play the timing and reaction will be restored. If the problem persists it will be best to wait until a practice session to work it out and restructure the correct response.

Individual Differences

Each player on the team is different from every other, in motive, personality, abilities, experience and physical attributes. This factor should be kept in focus in working with players to improve performance. The fact that people differ means that some will respond to one cue while some will respond to another. Some are shy, or timid, while others are aggressive. Some learn quickly while others will take some time to understand. The experience factor may affect how a player reacts in competition but some will learn to deal with this more quickly than others.

It is imperative that the coach learn to know all the team members not only for their playing capabilities, but also for their total personalities and their qualities as human beings. If this is done it will increase the probability that each player will improve more readily toward her potential, and will have a worthwhile experience in volleyball.

1. Corbin, Charles B. A *Textbook of Motor Development*. Dubuque: Wm. C. Brown Co., Pub., 1980.
2. Cratty, Bryant. *Movement Behavior and Motor Learning*. Philadelphia: Lea and Febiger, 1973.
3. Drowatzky, John N. *Motor Learning Principles and Practices*. Minneapolis: Burgess Publishing Co., 1975.
4. Gagne, Robert M. *Conditions of Learning*. New York: New York: Henry Holt and Co., 1977.
5. Knapp, Barbara. *Skill in Sport: The Attainment of Proficiency*. New York: Sportshelf, 1979.
6. Lawther, John D. *The Learning and Performance of Physical Skills*. Englewood Cliffs, New Jersey: Prentice Hall, Inc. 1977.
7. Magill, Richard. *Motor Learning Concepts and Application*. Dubuque: Wm. C. Brown Co., Pub. 1980.
8. Singer, Robert N. *Motor Learning and Human Performance*. New York: The Macmillan Co., 1975.
9. Zaichkowsky, Leonard D., Zaichkowsky, L. B., and Martinek, T. J. *Growth and Development—The Child and Physical Activity*. St. Louis: The C. V. Mosby Company, 1980.

Part Two

Individual Technical Skills

2

The Forearm Pass

The forearm pass (fig. 2.1), also known as the bump pass, is a method of passing the ball by bouncing it simultaneously off both forearms. The most common uses of the forearm pass include serve receiving, passing a hard spiked ball, and passing balls lower than the waist or away from the midline of the player's body.

Basic Technique

General Description

Ready position. As soon as possible the passer should move to a position in which the midline of her body is in line with the approaching ball. She should then place one foot slightly ahead of the other in a front-back stride position and flex at the knees and ankles to lower the buttocks toward the floor. Her arms are held away from her body at a 45° angle to the floor with elbows straight and hands clasped together.

Figure 2.1. The forearm pass.

Contact. Contact with the ball is made simultaneously on both forearms one to six inches above the wrists. Rather than swinging the arms to meet the ball the arms remain almost stationary as the legs extend to lift the body and arms up to the contact point. A slight forward shifting of the body weight accompanies the extension of the legs.

Follow-through. The follow-through consists of a continuation of the upward extension of the legs and a slight upward motion of the arms. The arms should not pass higher than the shoulders and the hands remain clasped until all upward movement ceases.

Footwork. Correct footwork is essential to good passing. Since opponents usually do not hit the ball directly at the passer she must assume a stance that allows her to move rapidly in any direction toward an approaching ball. The desired ready stance (fig. 2.2) on serve receive and free ball situations is: feet at least shoulder width apart; foot opposite intended direction of pass slightly ahead of the other; weight forward on balls of feet; arms in front of body, elbows easy and hands separated. The ready stance when a hard spike is anticipated should find the passer in a wider side stride with deeper knee flexion.

If a lateral movement to the ball is required the ready stance enables the passer to rapidly slide to near balls or turn and run to those further away. She is also in excellent position to step or run forward. Moving backward is possible but more difficult; however, if she is properly positioned on the court adjustments backwards are rarely necessary.

Once a position in line with the ball is achieved, a front-back stride position is desirable because it provides a broader base of support in the direction of the pass. The weight can be transferred forward into the pass without pulling the body's center of gravity beyond the front foot resulting in a loss of balance

Analysis of Performance Factors

Figure 2.2. Serve receive ready position.

and erratic passing. The amount of front-back stride position required depends on the distance the ball must be passed. In serve reception, particularly from the front half of the court, the pass has to travel only a few feet; therefore, little weight transfer is necessary and balance can be maintained with the feet almost parallel. On the other hand, a long cross-court pass requires a greater weight transfer and therefore one foot well ahead of the other.

Rebound surface. Few balls are carried or illegally hit when passed off the forearms. The forearms present a solid unjointed rebound surface to the ball. Upon contact the forearms hold their position while the ball compresses to absorb force. As a result the ball rebounds immediately from the forearms.

A good rebound surface is not only solid but as large and uniform as possible. A large rebound surface results in greater control because more of the ball is contacted making it easier to apply force through the center of the ball and to control the rebound.

The large, stable rebound surface is obtained by placing the hands together in such a manner to cause the fatty part at the base of the thumbs to touch and remain in contact throughout the forearm pass execution. Finger placement may vary depending upon the preferred technique.

The *interlocked* position (fig. 2.3) is created by interlocking the extended fingers with the thumbs in parallel position. In the *closed hand* position (fig. 2.4) one hand forms a fist to be grasped by the other hand. The thumbs are parallel and placed on top of the index fingers. The *open hand* position (fig. 2.5) is obtained by placing the back of one hand diagonally across the palm of the other hand. The fingers are curled with the thumbs in parallel position.

Once the hand position is assumed the wrists are then hyperextended, dropping the hands out of the way; the elbows are fully extended, placing the wrists side by side and the forearms almost parallel to one another. This should expose the wider, flatter inside surface of the forearms to the ball.

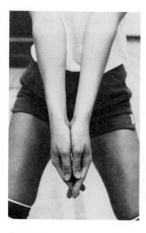

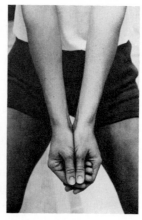

Figure 2.3. Interlock

Figure 2.4. Closed hand

Figure 2.5. Open hand.

Trajectory. The trajectory or rebound arc of the flight of the pass is determined by the angle at which the ball approaches the arms and the angle of the arms. Unless other factors are present, the angle at which the ball leaves the arms is equal and opposite to the angle from which the ball approached. For example, to pass a ball directly upward, which is descending straight down, the ball should be contacted at shoulder height with the arms extended parallel to the floor. To send the same ball diagonally forward and upward, the angle of the arms with the shoulder should be reduced slightly. On the other hand, a ball approaching from the other side of the net will go backwards when contacted with arms held parallel with the floor; it will go straight up when the angle of the arms at the shoulder is slightly less than parallel with the floor; and it will go back in the same trajectory at which it approached when the arms are held perpendicular with the path of the oncoming ball.

The problem of the passer is to position the arms so that the desired trajectory will result. Establishing the correct angle at contact is simplified if the arms are held away from the body at the desired angle as the player moves behind the ball and if this angle is not altered until the ball is passed. Even if the player misjudges the velocity of the ball and extends her legs too soon or too late, the rebound surface will be correctly angled. If the arms were allowed to swing up to meet the ball there is only one point in the arc of the swing in which the arms are correctly angled; swinging too soon results in a more vertical path than desired; too late sends the ball in too horizontal a plane. Therefore, an arm swing should not be used.

Changing direction of the pass. A majority of game situations require that the passer alter the line of the pass from that at which it approached her. If in the game situation the ball comes squarely at her and she wishes to pass the ball to her right, the change of direction is best accomplished by a step to the left away from the line of the approaching ball, followed by a pivot to a position squarely facing her target. Since the ball is a sphere she is in a position to apply force straightforwardly through the center of the ball in line with the target.

Passing a ball which is outside the line of the body. In some plays the passer may make every effort to get behind the ball, in line with her target, and still find the ball beyond her to her right or left. In this extreme situation she has no other choice than to reach outside the line of her body to pass the ball. When forced to do this she must raise the outside arm so that the combined forearm striking surface faces the target. This is, at best, a hazardous method of passing the ball. Force production through the ball in line with the target is difficult and control of the rebound angle is limited.

Common Errors—Cause and Correction

Following are errors commonly made in executing the forearm pass. Although listed separately many are interdependent and correction of one may eliminate or make possible the correction of several others.

The reader will also note that several of the errors produce the same results. An attempt has been made to categorize the errors according to basic result which is the first thing the coach may notice. It will often be necessary for the coach to use an elimination process to identify the cause.

Lack of Control—Rebound surface.

1. *Ball in hands.* Since a player has learned to catch a ball with her hands in other games this previous eyehand set frequently results in an attempt to play the ball with an open hand. The ball resting in the fingers or palms of hands as it is passed results in the ball being held (illegally) and a lack of control of the contact surface. This error can be eliminated by clasping the hands together, hyperextending the wrists, and practicing repeatedly to develop the reaction to passing the ball with the forearms.
2. *Ball contacted on hands.* Even though players know the hands should be clasped together and the ball contacted on the forearms many persist in passing the ball on their thumbs, wrists, or heels of the joined hands. This results in the ball traveling in unpredictable directions. The correction is to hyperextend the wrists to eliminate the hands as a rebound surface.
3. *Uneven forearms.* When one forearm is placed above the other either a double hit results or the ball contacts only the top arm. In the latter instance the path of the pass is usually off target to the right or the left. The correction is to clasp the hands together with one hand diagonally across the other. This allows the upper wrist to drop and levels the forearms.

Figure 2.6. Error: contacting ball on hands and wrists.

Figure 2.7. Error: one forearm higher than the other.

Figure 2.8. Error: player preparing to swing at ball.

4. *Swinging Arms.* Players at all levels are at times guilty of swinging the arms through the ball on the pass. This may result in a ball traveling too far or in an undesirable trajectory. The correction is to stabilize the arms at the desired passing angle and provide force through leg extension. Players should wait for the ball to drop down to their arms and then "meet," "nudge," "bump," or "bounce" the ball. Many players' passing improves if they actively attempt to shrug their shoulders as the only arm action.

Lack of control—Footwork and movement to ball.

1. *Ball too close to body.* The forearm pass should be contacted slightly further in front of the body than the overhand pass. Beginners frequently fail to make this distance adjustment and overrun the ball. Realizing they are too close they make one of the following adjustments.
   a. The body weight is shifted back away from the ball, followed by early extension of the legs and swinging of the arms, resulting in an early contact. The ball travels vertically or backward with very little power.
   b. The elbows are flexed to bring the forearms closer to the body. At best, this brings the forearms to a position parallel with the floor, sending the ball straight up. Oftentimes, the elbows are bent so much that the forearms face the player causing the ball to go back over the head or strike the player in the face.

Figure 2.9. Error: reaching laterally for ball.

c. The player may stand straight up and hold the arms stiffly against the body. The head is pulled back so the ball has room to drop. The ball is then allowed to hit where it may. If the player is extremely close to the ball a "chest" pass results. At best the ball will drop to the hands and shoot forward in a horizontal path.

The correction for all three problems is for the player to concentrate on the proper knee and hip flexion and to move so far behind the ball that she feels herself shifting her weight forward as she passes the ball.

2. *Reaching for ball.* Because of poor anticipation, reaction, or laziness, players frequently reach to either side to pass a ball (fig. 2.9) that could have been taken in line with the center of their bodies. The result is often a flat unplayable pass behind the player. Correction includes a correct starting stance with weight over the balls of the feet and the knees and hips flexed for a quick start from ready position. Concentrate on moving so that the ball is taken within the width of the stance.

3. *Moving with hands held together.* Moving laterally more than one step is hindered if the hands are clasped together in passing position. The correction is to move behind the ball with hands low and ready, and then clasp the hands together.

4. *Passing with straight legs.* Players often forget to bend the knees so they can be extended as a source of power. Straight-legged passers who compensate by swinging their arms at the ball lack control, while those whose arms remain stationary lack power or "carry" the ball on the arms which is illegal.

Figure 2.10. Error: feet in side-stride.

5. *Jumping at ball.* Jumping off the floor to pass the ball results in lack of control since adjustments while in the air are difficult. The player who jumps as the ball is contacted overpasses her target. The player who jumps up to meet the ball as soon as possible will lack power. The correct act is to wait for the ball to drop and then pass it.

6. *Feet in side-stride.* Passing from a parallel side-stride position (fig. 2.10) results in loss of balance if the ball is to be passed very far. Balance is also lost if a last minute adjustment to the flight of the ball is required. Correction consists of repeated practice and coaching in placing one foot ahead of the other in a variety of drills which require movement to the ball.

Although the technique and error corrections described above apply to most situations for the forearm pass, exceptional situations require further modification of the technique presented.

Forearm Pass Modifications

Examples of distance passing include the third pass from deep or outside the court, or a second hit recovery when the first pass has gone outside the playing court. In these situations the forearm pass technique must be modified to produce force at the potential expense of accuracy. This pass is executed as follows:

Distance Passing

The side is turned to the net to enable the arms to begin from as low a position as possible. The arms are swung upward and through the ball as the trunk rotates to contribute to the increase in power. Leg flexion and extension are the same as on a normal pass, although the full arm swing may cause the feet to leave the floor on follow-through.

Back Forearm Pass

If a perfect team existed its players would never be required to use a forearm pass to send the ball in a direction behind the passer. All less than perfect teams, however, create situations in which the passer is caught with her back to the target and the ball has dropped too low or is too far beyond her to be passed overhand. Since there is also insufficient time to run around the ball and face the target, the passer's sole play is to pass the ball off her forearms and hope it goes to the unseen target.

The backward trajectory is achieved by taking the ball slightly closer to the body than on the front forearm pass so that the back and neck can be arched and the ball passed off the forearms at a contact point higher than the shoulders.

Force is provided by flexion and extension of the legs, and on long passes the arms are swung at the ball. The greatest accuracy results when the back of the passer's hips and shoulders are square to the estimated location of the target. As long as the player contacts the ball evenly on both forearms the pass or set should be in line with the target. Since the target is not seen distance must also be estimated. Practice of this technique at varying distances from a target is necessary so that the player learns to estimate distance and alignment correctly.

Net Recovery

The forearm pass should be used when a recovery of a mispassed ball from the net is attempted. The player should *always* stand with her side to the net. This enables her to execute a pass in any direction and move rapidly toward or away from the net. If the net is tight, with a cable at the top and a cable or rope through the bottom, the resultant path of the ball can be anticipated. The player should be close to the net if the ball is headed for the extreme top or bottom of the net since the ball will fall in an extremely vertical path. However, if the ball is approaching the middle of the net the player should move

Figure 2.11. Net recovery.

a step or two off the net since the ball will tend to bounce out somewhat. The greater the velocity of the approaching ball the further it will rebound from any part of the net.

The secret of a successful net recovery lies in taking the ball as low to the floor as possible. If the ball must be sent over the net the net becomes less of an obstacle the lower the ball drops because the horizontal component of its trajectory takes it further from the net. Even if the ball falls straight down out of the net and must be sent over the net, by crouching low the passer gains time to judge the correct forearm angle and amount of top spin necessary to send the ball over the net.

When the forearm pass is utilized for the purpose of recovering a hard spiked ball it is referred to as a dig. A complete analysis of the dig, dive and roll techniques will be covered in Chapter 6 titled Individual Defense.

Passing a Hard Spiked Ball

1. Practice procedures should be organized so that all players are actively involved as much of the time as possible.
2. In most drills players should work in no more than twos, threes, or fours. There should be enough balls so that one is available to every two players.
3. It is important to be aware of the pace of practice. Each player should receive adequate time for practice. Rotate players on time, and move efficiently from one practice procedure to the next.
4. Players should know what the drill is for and be aware of the specific demands for relating it to a game situation.
5. Attempt to utilize the techniques practiced in a game situation relatively soon after isolated technique practice.
6. The coach should try to see each player perform, using cue words for assistance. If the group as a whole has a problem, re-explain to everyone. If one player has difficulty, arrange for individual work, but keep the team moving in purposeful practice while individual coaching takes place.

Suggested Practice Procedures for the Forearm Pass

Preparation and Use

Practice Progressions

Purpose	Description and Specifications
Basic Technique	Two players, one ball. Tosser lobs high, soft pass to partner. Concentrate on stance, angle of arms, getting force with legs, trajectory of pass.
Lateral Movement and Footwork (Ball-Target Relationship)	Two players, one ball. Tosser lobs soft pass to right and left. Concentrate on lateral stride, getting squarely behind the ball in relation to target (tosser).

Purpose	Description and Specifications
Movement Forward and Back, Choice of Pass, Calling	Three players, one ball. One player (leader) faces two in semicircle. Leader uses overhand pass, places ball to any player, short, overhead. Player must use overhand pass whenever possible, forearm pass when necessary. Concentrate on ready position (feet and hands), footwork, calling balls between players.
Changing Direction, Accuracy	Three players, one ball. Players form a triangle. 1 tosses lob pass to 2; 2 forearm passes to 3; 3 catches and tosses to 1; 1 forearm passes to 2, etc. Concentrate turning to squarely face spot in front of next player (target), height of flight of pass, 10–15 feet.
Reaction to Speed of Flight and Lateral Movement	1. Two players, one ball. Combine with lateral movement to squarely face target (partner). Partner places ball 2–3 feet to either side. 2. Three players, 6 balls. Player 1 serves the ball deep between players 2 and 3 who are aligned in the deep positions of a **W** receive formation. Players call the ball and pass the serve to a designated target. The drill continues until the passers have 10 good passes. Players then rotate positions.
Distance	Three players, two balls. Players space so that 1 is on rear court, 2 is midcourt, and 3 is across the net. 2 tosses high over 1's right or left shoulder; 1 hits ball to 3 with side to net.

Purpose	Description and Specifications
Backward Pass	Same as distance passing, except 1 starts inside court, 2 tosses flat arc pass, and 3 is on same side of net as blind target.
Team "Hustle"	Three players, one ball. 1 at net, 2 and 3 in rear court area. 1 tosses ball far off court at side or rear. 2 and 3 move to ball together. Whichever one can get to ball does so, as other player moves with her attempting to anticipate direction and flight of recovery, setting recovery back to 1. Encourage recovery players to call, "Mine," "I'm with you," etc.

3

The Overhand Pass

The overhand pass (fig. 3.1) is the most accurate method of playing the ball. However, it is also the technique with the highest incidence of illegal ball contacts or "throws."

The use of the overhand pass is restricted to situations in which the passer has time to assume a balanced, well-aligned position behind the ball and in line with the intended target. Examples of such situations include passing a free ball and setting a ball after it has first been passed into the air by a teammate. However, it may also be used in trouble or save situations when the passer is certain her alignment with the ball will allow her to contact it legally.

Basic Technique

General Description

Ready position. Perhaps the most important phase of the overhand pass technique is assuming a ready position that places the passer behind the ball and the ball in direct alignment with the midline of the passer's body and the target. Once this alignment is achieved the player should assume a front-back stride position in which one foot leads the other by at least eight inches. The knees should be flexed with the weight evenly distributed between both feet (fig. 3.1). The wrists are hyperextended and the relaxed fingers point diagonally upward while the thumbs point toward each other. This creates a triangle

Figure 3.1. The overhand pass (side view).

formed by the thumbs and forefingers. The elbows are rotated out away from the midline of the body. From this position the passer should be able to see the back of her hands and the approaching ball. Figure 3.1 illustrates this clearly.

Figure 3.2. The overhand pass (front view).

Contact. The fingers should contact the ball six to eight inches off the forehead. Contact should be made on all fingers with the primary force supplied through the thumb and the first two fingers of each hand while the remaining fingers act to guide the ball as it is released.

Prior to contact the legs should begin to extend slightly. As the ball is contacted, extension of the legs continues and extension of the elbows and wrists begins. Extension of the legs, arms, and wrist continues as rapidly as possible until the ball is released. Illustrations in Figures 3.1, 3.2, and 3.7 show the ball as if caught. Actually this occurs so fast the eye cannot see it.

Follow-through. After release the hands follow the ball until complete arm extension is effected. At this point the wrists should be in extension and the fingers either extended or relaxed into a slightly flexed position. The legs should be completely extended with both heels off the floor and most of the body weight shifted to the front foot.

Footwork. The importance of moving to proper alignment with the ball cannot be overemphasized. Because the hands are not joined and are, therefore, capable of independent action, an alignment which requires one hand to execute an action different from the other hand usually produces unequal contact time or force application between the two hands. As a result, the ball is either misdirected or hit illegally in a "throw" or double hit. An example of this is moving to the ball so that it is contacted in line with the right shoulder instead of the midline of the body. If the hands act equally on the ball, the pass, although legal, will be to the right rather than forward. If a forward pass is attempted the ball will rest too long in the right hand because it is too far away from the midline of the body to utilize arm or leg extension, and the left hand cannot get far enough behind the ball to produce a forward force component.

The problem of changing the direction of the approaching ball is even more acute in the overhand pass than the forearm pass, although the solution is the same. Once again if the ball is to be passed to the right of the path of the approaching ball, the player must step to her left and pivot so that her shoulders are square to target of the pass. This movement must be effected before the ball is contacted; turning on the ball as it is passed results in an illegally long contact with the outside hand.

The wrists acting alone can produce only enough force to pass the ball a very short distance. Therefore, the feet must be in front-back stride position to allow weight to shift forward as the legs and arms extend. The further the ball must be passed, the wider the front-back stride must be.

Hand action. The hand position, forming a triangle with wrists hyperextended, is important. The top of the triangle may be opened slightly, but if the bottom is allowed to open, the hands are placed in a very weak position. From this weakened position the thumbs are easily "jammed" if the ball should be misjudged or if top spin causes the ball to drop lower than anticipated. In these instances, if the thumbs are together, the ball will simply be a "carry" or will hit the palms, but injury will not occur.

Skilled players use two different methods of hand action in the overhead pass. In the first, the elbows are wrists begin to extend ever so slightly prior to contact and then extend fully with contact. This causes the ball to appear to be "flicked" on the pass. In the second method, the elbows and wrists retract slightly on contact and then extend fully into the release. In description it might be construed that in this method the ball is caught. In actuality, the action occurs so fast it cannot be clearly perceived and the ball is legally volleyed.

Theoretically, the second major method should produce greater accuracy because the ball is in contact with the surface slighly longer. Skilled players range in movement patterns between the extremes of both methods with varying degrees of success.

Trajectory. Most strategic situations require a ball to be passed diagonally forward and up into the air. The only place the fingers can be faced both forward and upward while the wrists are hyperextended and the hands close together is in front of the face. If the hands were taken down at the last minute, the ball should contact the passer on her nose (fig. 3.1, frame 2), although her perception would be that the ball was approaching her forehead.

If the passer contacts the ball lower than her face it is almost impossible to legally pass the ball in an upward trajectory because it is difficult for hands to be turned upward at this level from an overhand position.

If a passer gets too close to the ball so that it is contacted over the crown of her head her fingers will face more upward than forward and the ball will travel straight up.

The player who attempts to put more force into her overhand passes by flexing the wrists as she contacts the ball destroys the upward angle of the fingers; a flat or downward trajectory will result. The pass may also be illegal if the ball remains in contact with the fingers too long.

Lack of power.

Common Errors— Cause and Correction

1. *Elbows extended as ball contacted.* Extending the elbows before the ball is contacted stops the sequential addition of body parts in producing force, resulting in a weak pass. It also faces the fingers forward resulting in a very flat pass. The player must wait for the ball to drop so that it can be contacted six to eight inches in front and above her nose. Repeated practice in moving into position for a pass, allowing the ball to drop and then catching it with proper hand position, may help to develop this concept.
2. *Insufficient leg flexion.* Leg extension is a major source of power in the overhand pass. If the legs are not flexed they cannot be extended and a weak pass results. Players should be coached to bend the knees and given practice in moving and then passing. Practice in a stationary position many times encourages lack of leg action. Running and sliding drills in which a player is not allowed to fully extend the legs may also create an awareness of how it feels to flex the knees.
3. *Side stride.* Particularly when forced to back up to pass a ball, many players are guilty of passing with their feet parallel to each other in a side

Figure 3.3. Error: feet in side stride.

stride position. This may result in weak passes or loss of power. Coaching and repeated practice in assuming a front-back stride position are necessary.

4. *Jumping at the ball.* Jumping at the ball may be the cause of other passing errors. Players who jump before the ball is contacted lose rather than gain power. They also tend to pass the ball in a low trajectory because the jump carries the nose above the ball before contact. Players who extend the elbows too soon often jump at the ball to attempt to make up for lost power. Jumping can usually be cured by taking a deeper knee bend and concentrating on pushing smoothly away from the floor with the toes maintaining contact.

Lack of control.

1. *Ball contacted lower than nose.* A ball contacted below the level of the nose results in very flat or illegal pass. The correction is repeated practice on footwork in order to get to the ball properly and to concentrate on flexing the knees.

2. *Taking ball too close to body.* If the ball is passed from a position over the crown of the head it usually goes straight up. If the player steps away from the ball so that she can contact it in front of her face her body weight works against her and the pass is weak. Again, practice moving to the ball laterally, both forward and back is necessary, so that the player can learn to perceive the correct position.

Figure 3.4. Error: ball contacted at low level.

Figure 3.5. Error: contacting ball above head.

Figure 3.6. Error: stepping away from pass.

3. *Taking ball to right or left of midline of body.* Passing the ball from a position right or left of the midline of the body may result in a mispassed or poorly directed pass. Practice which concentrates on lateral running or sliding and turning to the target should be done to correct this error.

4. *Turning on ball as it is passed.* Attempting to give a new direction to the ball while it is being contacted results in an illegal pass. This is usually a result of facing the direction of the oncoming pass and waiting until the last moment to turn to face the target. Practice is necessary so that the player aways faces the potential target and utilizes side slides or cross-over running steps to get to the ball while still facing the target.

5. *Passing on the run.* Passing from other than a stationary position may result in illegally pushing the ball or over-passing the target. The player should begin her move for the ball sooner; if she is still late, she should pass the ball with the forearms. The players should practice movement drills, concentrating on planting the feet in proper position prior to each pass.

6. *Flexing wrists.* The player whose wrists are flexed on follow-through probably has mispassed the ball, and the trajectory of the pass was probably flat. Drill is necessary in catching the ball in proper hand position, followed by concentration on passing with hands going from hyperextension to extension.

7. *Pulling hands back from pass.* Some players pull their hands back toward the body as soon as they contact the ball in the belief that this will keep them from contacting the ball too long. Instead, it may result in a weak pass or misdirected pass. Coach for a complete follow-through. The total body follows the ball, including hands.

8. *Jabbing at ball with fingers.* Players told to pass the ball with their fingertips sometimes interpret this to mean the ends of their fingers should provide the contact surface. Thus they jab at the ball like they were trying to pass on the ends of ten pencil points. The contact surface is so small and wrist action so poor that the pass is weak or misdirected. Fingernails may also be broken. It may be necessary to reestablish the concept that the ball is passed on the inside surfaces of the last two joints of the fingers. Much practice will be necessary to correct this error.

9. *One hand leading.* Some players consistently follow through with one hand ahead of the other. Frequently it is the dominant hand, or it may be the hand corresponding to their lead foot. The result is usually a pass off-target in the direction opposite the leading hand. Correction includes increasing strength and coordination of the nondominant hand and leading with the foot opposite the dominant hand.

Setting

The most frequent use of the overhand technique is to set the ball up into the air close to the net for the spike. Although the ball could also be set with a forearm pass, the accuracy and consistency necessary are best achieved with the overhand technique. The forearm set should be used only when an all-out effort to get to the ball has been made and the ball has dropped too low to be taken overhand.

Front Set Technique

The technique for the front set is essentially the same as the overhand pass. The major difference is that, when passing, either foot may lead in the required front-back stride position. When setting, the foot nearest the net should lead. This keeps the shoulder nearest the net from turning toward it, helping to prevent an "overset," or set that crossed on to the opponent's side of the net. Oversets usually result in easy points for the opponents.

The setter's footwork must be precise. She should get to the pass in time to get set, facing the direction of her pass in perfect alignment with the ball. If the ball is passed short and she is forced to move away from the net to reach it, she should sidestep to reach the ball, keeping her shoulders square to the desired direction of the set.

The majority of sets should be executed from a position in the front third and center of the court by a player with good hands designated as the setter. However, if the pass is too far from the setter the nearest player should call for the ball and set it. The distance and arc of a set vary with the strategic requirements of the play, the ability of the spiker, and the accuracy of the pass.

Figure 3.7. Back set.

Figure 3.8. Error: contacting ball too far back.

Good strategy often requires the setter to set the ball to a spiker behind her to deceive the opposing blocker.

Back Set Technique

To prevent the opponents from anticipating the back set, the setter's body position and contact point should be identical to that used in the front set. Upon contact the setter arches her back and neck which directs the set backward over her head while the palms face upward on the follow-through. As the legs are extended the hips shift toward with weight evenly distributed over both feet. If the ball is taken too far behind the head only the fingertips will be below the ball and the set will roll off the fingers into an unplayable flat arc.

Jump Set Technique When the pass is long or tight to the net it requires the setter to adjust her position by leaping upward off both feet to make contact with the ball before it travels over or into the net. Basic setting techniques used in the front and back sets are used in the jump set with the exception of the feet being in the air at the point of contact. The jump set can be used strategically by highly skilled players as a means of confusing the opposing block.

Setting Variations *Six-set* or *Regular set* (Figure 3.9, set 6). The ball is set just inside the sideline tape, one to two feet away from the net with the highest point in its vertical arc six to ten feet above the net. The regular set is designed to take advantage of a weak blocker and is the highest percentage set when the ball is inaccurately passed to the setter.

Play Sets. Play sets are sets other than the regular set with the high vertical trajectory. Play sets remain in the air less time than the regular set and are designed to alter the pattern and speed of play.

Play sets are identified by various names, letters and numbers. The terms presented are those commonly used, however the coach should designate the plays in whatever way is most meaningful to her players and easiest to call out during play.

1. *One-set* or *Japanese set* (Figure 3.9, set 1) The ball is set inches above the net and is contacted by the setter after the spiker has jumped into the air. The spiker reaches the top of her jump as the ball clears the net. The one-set is designed to beat the opposing blockers with quickness of execution, and often holds the middle blocker on the floor.
2. *Two-set* (Figure 3.9, set 2). the ball is set two to three feet above the net and requires the spiker to begin her approach just before the ball is set and her take off immediately after the set. The two-set does not require the precision timing of the one-set because of the increased height of the set. It is designed to hold the middle blocker and create a one-on-one blocking situation.
3. *Three-set* (Figure 3.9, set 3). The ball is set one to three feet above the net to a point seven to eight feet from the sideline. The three-set requires the spiker to jump into the air before the ball is contacted by the setter. The three-set is designed to attack the space between the outside and middle blocker by attacking the ball before the block forms.
4. *Four set or Shoot set* (Figure 3.9, set 4). The ball is set low and fast to the outside spiker to a point about one foot from the sideline at a height of one to two feet above the net. The four-set is designed to attack the space between the outside and middle blocker by attacking the ball before the middle blocker can close the block.

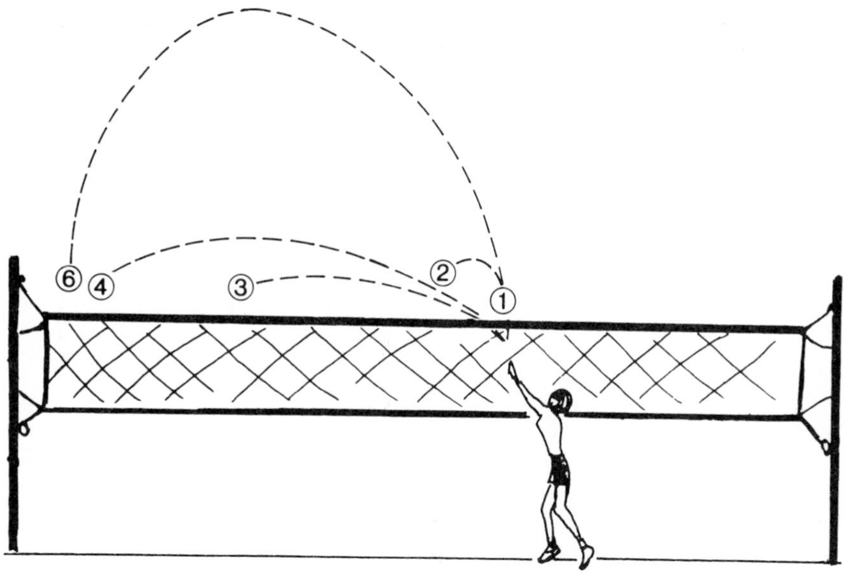

Figure 3.9. Setting heights for regular set (6) and play sets (1, 2, 3, 4).

The setter is the "quarterback" of the team; she determines when and how the offense will form. Factors that should be considered when setting include the following:

Decisions in Setting

Beginning level.

1. Set wider to the off-hand spiker than the on-hand spiker.
2. Assuming both players are right-handed and of equal ability, set the on-hand spiker more often than the off-hand spiker.
3. If one spiker is greatly superior to the other, know where she is and give her the majority of the sets.
4. Never set exclusively to one spiker, ignoring the other spiker completely. This will eliminate any element of surprise and allow the defense to key on the strong spiker, making her less effective than she otherwise might be.
5. If a spiker is left-handed, remember where she is on the court. When she is on the left side of the court, she is on her off-hand side; she is on-hand when on the right side of the court.
6. Attempt a back set only on a good pass. When in trouble make the easy set to the spiker you are facing.
7. Do not often back set to an off-hand spiker unless she is a strong player.
8. Do not attempt a back set more than half the width of the cout.
9. If a spiker has missed or hit two or more consecutive spikes into the block, set the other spiker.
10. Remember to cover the spiker on a bad set. Showing disgust with the set by standing and watching will not help to save the point.

Intermediate Level.

1. Know the preferences of your spikers. Spikers with fast approaches usually need a set slightly lower than normal. Slow moving spikers or extremely tall spikers require sets a little higher than normal.
2. Set the ball further off the net for short spikers.
3. Know the location of any exceptionally tall or short blockers on the opposite team. Whenever possible, set over the short blocker and away from the tall blocker.
4. Know which spikers are having good and bad days. The spiker who is on her game should receive many sets, including those in which the setter is off balance.
5. When your setting is off, attempt simple sets and do not try to put the ball too close to the net.

Advanced level—using multiple offense.

1. Do not attempt a shoot, two, or other play set if the pass is bad.
2. If the spiker calls for a play set too late or when she is out of position, set someone else.
3. Set all spikers early in the game. This lets the opponents know that you intend to use everyone and therefore they must block one on one until the direction of the set is apparent.
4. Utilize the center set often enough to hold the middle blocker.
5. Talk to your spiker. If you see a play that should be tried, suggest that the spiker call it. If the ball is set over her short blocker and she insists on hitting into the tall one, suggest the obvious alternative. However, the setter should not attempt to play coach on the court and attempt to analyze her spiker's technical errors.

Suggested Practice Procedures for the Overhand Pass

Preparation and Use

1. Practice procedures should be organized so that all players are actively involved as much of the time as possible.
2. In most drills players should work in no more than twos, threes, or fours. There should be enough balls so that one is available to every two players.
3. It is important to be aware of the pace of practice. Each player should receive adequate time for practice; rotate players on time and to move efficiently from one practice procedure to the next.
4. Players should know what the drill is for and be aware of the specific demands for relating it to a game situation.
5. Attempt to utilize the techniques practiced in a game situation relatively soon after isolated technique practice.
6. The coach should try to see each player perform, using cue words for assistance. If the group as a whole has a problem reexplain to everyone. If one player has difficulty, arrange for individual work, but keep the team moving in purposeful practice while individual coaching takes place.

Purpose
Basic Technique

Description and Specifications
Two players, one ball. Spaced at a distance of 8–10 feet. Players assume stance and pass with high, soft arc. Concentrate on feet, arms, hand position. Aim ball so top of arc is halfway to partner.

Footwork, Body Control
  Controlling Momentum.

Three players, one ball. 2 lines up behind 1. 3 faces 1. One passes to 3 and moves to the right to take 3's place; 3 passes to 2 and moves to the right to take 2's place, etc. Players must remember that as one moves to the ball the momentum of the body will be transferred to the ball, affecting control. Catch all bad passes and start over. (fig. 3.10)

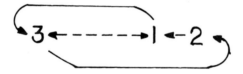

Figure 3.10.
Footwork and ball control.

Lateral Movement to the Ball,
  Footwork and Ball-target
  Relationship.

1. Two players, one ball. 1 passes ball alternately 2–4 feet to either side of 2. 2 slides sidewards, turning to squarely face 1 with body directly behind ball (fig. 3.11).

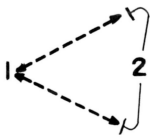

Figure 3.11. Lateral movement.

Purpose

Description and Specifications

2. Three players, one ball. Players form a triangle. 1 tosses ball directly in front of herself to either of the spots designated in Figure 2.12; 2, while facing 3 with the upper body, runs to a point behind the ball using cross-over running steps and passes the ball to 3. Players reposition and 3 tosses for 1, etc. Change direction to work on movement to other side.

Figure 3.12. Lateral movement, footwork.

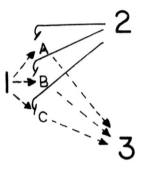

Change of Direction

Four players, one ball. Players form a square (fig. 3.13). Facing counterclockwise, 1 passes ball to a spot in front of 2, 2 passes to a spot in front of 3, etc. Players receiving the pass should face the direction from which the ball is coming. Concentrate on staying behind the line to which the passer is facing.

Figure 3.13. Change of direction.

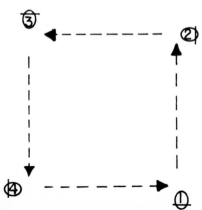

Purpose	**Description and Specifications**
Distance	Two players, one ball. Start 8–10 feet apart. Progressively move back. As distance increases, concentrate on making the top of pass arc further forward. Get added force by pushing hard off the floor after contact.
Setting Placement	Three players, one ball. 1 starts at CF facing center of court about one foot from net with hands above head. 2 lob tosses to 1, 1 sets ball to drop into 3's hands, with ball traveling to height of 12–15 feet above the court (2 × 7′4″ net height as guide). Reverse to other side of court.
Movement to Ball	1. Review lateral movement to ball #2 above. 2. Three player, one ball. Position as shown in Figure 3.14. 1 starts at position A; 3 tosses lob to spots A, B, or C; 1 sets toward 2 who catches ball. Reverse to other side of court.

Figure 3.14. Setter's movement.

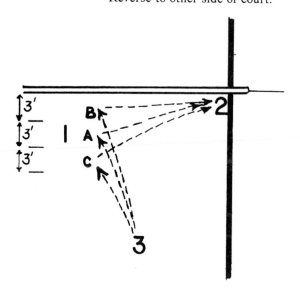

Purpose	Description and Specifications
Back Set	Three players, one ball. 1 stands on left sideline facing center, 3 stands on right sideline facing center court, 2 is at center court facing 1, all are 1–2 feet from net. 1 front sets to 2, 2 back sets to 3 and turns to face 3, etc. The same pattern can be done using rear cout line as a net guide.
Backcourt Set	Three players, two balls. 3 tosses lob pass in front of 1. 1 pushes set toward diagonally opposite net post, 2 catches ball (fig. 3.15).

Figure 3.15.
Backcourt set.

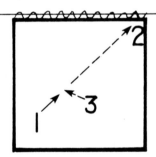

Cross-Court Set	Three players, one ball. 3 tosses lob pass in front of 1, 1 pushes set cross court, parallel to net to 2 on opposite side of court. The same pattern can be done using rear court line as net guide (fig. 3.16).

Figure 3.16. Cross-court set.

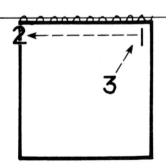

Purpose	**Description and Specifications**
Combinations	1. *Choice of spikers.* Any of the spiking drills can be organized with more than one spiking line. From a toss to the setter, she practices the choice of set variations as appropriated.
	2. *Endurance and movement.* In the spiking endurance drill the same setter repeatedly sets 10–20 sets to the same spiker who must spike, recover, spike, recover in rapid succession. To work, the setter must continually move to the ball.
Team Coordination	1. *Calling.* Often the first hit is between the setter and another player (CB, RB or LB). To coordinate, right-of-way and calling practice can be organized with the setter and any of the backcourt players in position. A tosser lobs the ball high between the two players. Both must move to the ball, one calls the other off, and make an accurate set to the spiker that player is facing. This can be done with spiking lines at both RF and LF with spikers practicing hitting. The depth to which a setter will be allowed to go to bad passes should be determined by her speed and experience.
	2. *Covering the hitter.* In all spiking drills combined with blocking, the setter must practice covering the spiker following her set.

4

The Attack

After the ball has been served, the spike becomes the primary offensive technique in volleyball. It is also more complex, although not necessarily more difficult, than other volleyball techniques. The spike consists of an approach to the ball, a vertical jump, and a striking of the ball with the hand above the net height to send the ball forcefully downward into the opponent's court. This technique is shown in Figure 1. A spiker on the side of the court with her hitting hand on the same side of her body as the approaching set is called the "on-hand spiker." This is the left front position for a right-handed spiker. Conversely, a spiker whose hitting hand is on the side of her body opposite the approaching set is an "off-hand" spiker. This is the right front position for a right-handed player. All descriptions in this chapter refer to movement for the right-handed spiker.

Figure 4.1. The spike.

Ready position. As soon as the spiker sees that she will not have to set the ball she should move to the ready position for the spike. If she is the left or right front she should move toward the closer sideline, eight to ten feet from the net. The on-hand spiker should be one to two feet outside the sideline. The off-hand spiker should be on the sidelines or one foot outside the sideline. The spiker's feet should point toward the net although her shoulders should be turned so that she can see the setter. Her weight should be on the balls of her feet with her hands in front of her.

The ready position described above makes an approach to the set possible. An approach is desirable because it enables the spiker to jump higher by converting her forward momentum, built up as she approaches the ball, into upward momentum. The ready position also insures that the spiker will be moving forward to spike the set since only a very poor set would be further back from the net than her ready position.

Basic Technique

General Description

Figure 4.2. The step-close approach to the spike.

Approach. There are only two spiking approach footwork patterns used by consistently successful spikers. Both employ a two-foot takeoff, but differ in footwork prior to takeoff.

The *step-close* approach, as shown in figure 4.2, consists of an initial forward step with the left foot, then a stride on to the right foot, followed immediately by a closing third step with the left foot. The relative timing of the three steps is slow, slow, fast. This is the approach used by a majority of players in the United States.

The hop approach, as shown in Figure 4.3, may be preceded by one or more steps, but begins with a step onto the left foot. The player then jumps off the left foot into the air and lands simultaneously on the heels of both feet. The hop approach is used less frequently in the United States than the step-close approach, although it is used exclusively in some countries by outstanding volleyball teams.

Beginners may have difficulty learning either of the approach patterns. Regardless of the approach attempted, it must be practiced many times without the ball before successful execution of the complete spike is possible.

The decision as to which footwork pattern to use is not easy. The step-close provides greater opportunity for last minute adjustments because determination of take-off position is not completely made until the third step. In the hop, the take-off position is pre-determined as soon as the body jumps off the left foot. The advantage of the hop is that the player approaches the ball faster. This facilitates her in moving to a ball set inside or too low. It also makes play sets more effective because the spiker does not give them away by starting her approach early. One approach may be more suited to the natural jumping rhythm of the player than the other, and should be considered by the coach and player in determining the most effective technique.

The arms also are imortant in the approach. As the spiker is moving forward her arms swing from an initial position in front of her body rapidly downward, back, and up until her hands are actually higher than her shoulders as

Figure 4.3. The hop approach to the spike.

Figure 4.4. The spike: take off and backswing.

both heels approach the floor on the hop approach or the right heel reaches for the floor on the step-close approach. As the heel(s) dig in the knees flex and the arms swing down toward the floor, effectively curbing the forward momentum and preparing the body for its flight upward. This can be seen in both Figures 4.2 and 4.3.

Jump. The body is propelled upward by the forceful extension of the legs and ankles combined with the rapid forward and upward movement of the arms. As the arms extended forward at shoulder height the elbows flex and both hands continue upward. After the elbow of the striking arm reaches shoulder height the striking hand and arm swing back and away from the net. The elbow remains high while the shoulder rotates back as far as possible. The back arches and the legs flex slightly. This sequence is shown in Figure 4.4.

Contact. The forward movement of the striking hand is initiated by allowing gravity to pull the nondominant hand downward. The elbow leads the hyperextended wrist toward the ball. As the elbow straightens, the wrist begins to extend forcefully. The ball is contacted by the heel of the hand as the wrist continues rapidly forward into flexion. The heel of the hand makes the initial contact, followed immediately by the rest of the opened hand.

Follow-through. The follow-through varies depending on where the ball is directed. In all instances, however, the player lands simultaneously on the toes of both feet or the left and then the right. Her landing is cushioned by flexing at the ankles and knees.

Analysis of Performance Factors

The approach. The approach varies with the quality of the set. On a correctly executed regular set the side spiker should wait until the ball has been set and then make her approach toward the anticipated point of contact with the ball. However, if she judges that the regular set is too high she must wait longer before beginning her approach. If the set is too low or pulled inside she must start toward the ball as soon as she knows where it is going. When pulled inside on the off-hand side, the side spiker must remember to take an extra step toward the middle of the court so the ball comes across her body and is contacted in front of the shoulder of her striking hand.

When attempting to strike a backcourt set the spiker should turn so that her feet are at a 90° angle with the expected path of the set. She must hold her approach until the ball reaches a point between her and the net, then rapidly approach the ball.

When spiking a "two" set the spiker must begin her approach a little before the ball leaves the setter's hands. However, when hitting a "shoot" or "three" set the spiker must begin her approach well before the ball is set. The spiker should approach the "shoot" set by running toward the net post until she is two to three feet from the net, then turn and approach the ball moving parallel to the net. On the "three" set the spiker should approach the anticipated point of contact at a shallow angle almost parallel with the net.

The center spiker has an additional approach problem when the pass pulls the setter out of her usual right-of-center position at the net. If the pass pulls the setter directly in front of the center spiker, in order to spike a center set wthout running into the setter, she must move laterally either to the left for a front set or to the right for a backset. Which way she moves is not as important as her moving early enough that the setter knows where she is.

Producing power. Any time the body is used in producing force, as many body segments as possible should be used in a continuous sequence to insure maximum power. Often the spiker will attempt to get all the power for the hit with the arm. The upper body should also be used. To develop this, rotation of the shoulders and hyperextension and flexion of the trunk are utilized.

Figure 4.5. On-hand down-the-line spike.

Figure 4.6. On-hand cross-court spike.

Shoulder rotation increases power on the on-hand side by lengthening the backswing of the hitting arm. Off-hand power is increased when hitting cross court by shoulder rotation which helps bring the arm across the body. In both instances body rotation is facilitated by a takeoff at a slight angle to the net, facing the setter. The turn in preparation for the full body hit is also facilitated by aiming the left hand at the ball as the arms lift for the jump.

To get maximum power the arm should move through the longest arc possible. This can only be accomplished if the body is fully rotated into the back-swing and the arm is fully extended into the hit. The length of the follow-through is limited only by the nearness to the net. Examples of the follow-through adjustments are shown in Figures 4.5 and 4.6, respectively.

Figure 4.7. Off-hand down-the-line spike.

Giving direction to the spike. Regardless of where the ball is set, the spiker should always attempt to position herself so that when she is in the air and swinging forward, the ball is in line with and slightly closer to the net than the shoulder of her hitting hand (fig. 4.5, frame 3). She should also feel square to the net in the sense that if she were to swing straightforward her hips and shoulders would be parallel to the net (fig. 4.5, frame 3) upon contacting the ball.

To be effective a spiker must be able to control the direction of her spike. To be most effective she should disguise the intended path of her spike as long as possible. This is possible if, and only if, she aligns herself behind the ball as described above.

There are three basic movement patterns the spiker is called upon to execute. The first, the down-the-line spike, is relatively easy on the onhand side. Assuming good alignment with the ball, the player need only to swing her hand straightforward through he ball (fig. 4.5). The of-hand down-the-line shot, although basically the same movement, is more difficult. Timing and position problems are greater because the spiker must wait for the ball to cross her body to her spiking side (fig. 4.7). Also, the amount of power producing shoulder rotation is limited by the need to look in the opposite direction from the shoulder in order to watch the ball.

The second movement pattern is the on-hand cross court. The on-hand cross court to the middle of the court is relatively easy; therefore, it is the most commonly hit angle at beginning and intermediate levels. The sharp on-hand cross-court angle toward the opposite sideline is much more difficult to execute (fig. 4.6). However, its use increases at advanced levels because the block usually takes away the middle of the court. Regardless of how far toward the sideline the ball is to be hit, the on-hand cross-court spike should proceed like any other until the body is in the air and the striking hand begins its backswing. At this time the spiker's trunk should twist from the hips up, allowing the head and the spiking hand to take a position behind the ball. The forward motion of the arm consists of the shoulder, elbow, and arm swinging diagonally

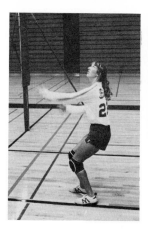

through the center of the ball from the player's left to her right. On very sharp cross-court hits, the spiker's shoulder and striking arm feel like they are working in opposition to one another; the shoulder leads forward while the arm travels in a plane at lateral right angle to the motion of the shoulder.

The third movement, the off-hand cross-court hit is the easiest to hit from the off-hand spiking side because the hand follows the shoulder forward and is helped as it comes across the body and the ball by the trunk turning with it (fig. 4.8).

Figure 4.8. Off-hand cross-court spike.

Angle of hand on ball at contact. Almost all spikes should be hit with top spin. Top spin is created by applying force to the ball off-center in an upward and forward direction (fig. 4.9). This increases the downward trajectory of the spike. A spike contacted well above and close to the net requires less top spin

A. Initial contact.   B. Hand coming over the ball.

Figure 4.9. Hand action in applying top spin to the spike.

Figure 4.10.
Trajectory of the spike hit with top spin at varying distances from the net.

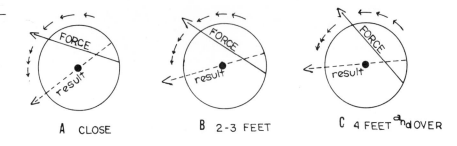

A CLOSE   B 2-3 FEET   C 4 FEET and OVER

to keep it in the court because the spiker contacts the ball toward the top and is able to hit down on the ball (fig. 4.10A). A normal set two to three feet off the net requires the spiker to contact the base of the ball with the heel of her hand and send her fingers over the ball to produce top spin and a downward trajectory (fig. 4.10B). When the ball is set several feet off the net it can still be spiked over providing the spiker hits up into the ball, contacting it above her head, toward the bottom of the ball, and rapidly flipping her wrist and fingers up the back of the ball (fig. 4.10C). A short spiker can use the latter technique to "spike" the ball even though she cannot reach as high as the top of the net.

Common Errors— Cause and Correction

Because spiking is a very complex technique, the causes and effects of many errors are interrelated. For this reason it should be noted that the same causes may be repeated under two categories of error effects.

Lack of body control in approach.

1. *One foot takeoff.* Many beginners attempt to take off on one foot, usually their left. This causes them to turn on the ball, sending it to their left. Their forward momentum often continues after they jump, resulting in a net foul. The correction is to learn either the jump-to-two-feet or the stride-close approach. The two foot takeoffs make it easier to control the rotation of the body because of the greater balance afforded by the wider base of support.
2. *Broad jumping.* Broad jumping, or taking off well back from the net and jumping forward into it, is usually a result of landing on the toes rather than the heels prior to takeoff. Work must be done to keep the center of gravity behind the base of support as the two feet contact for the jump. This will assure that the body can be controlled into the upward thrust. Correction is often facilitated by practicing the takeoff facing and a few feet back from a wall.

Figure 4.11. Error: one-foot takeoff.

Lack of height in the jump.

1. *Approaching too soon.* A player commonly will be so anxious to spike the ball that she begins her approach too soon. This gets her to the net before the ball. If she goes ahead and jumps, she will come down before the ball does. If the player waits for the ball, all momentum will be lost and the jump will be lower. If the ball is set back off the net, she will have to run backwards to hit it. The player must be coached to wait. A cue that may help is to "wait until the ball is off the setter's hands." This will allow the spiker to see the initial movement of the ball and make adjustments to set placement. It also approximates the appropriate time to start, though each player must learn to adapt to her own body speed and the height of the set. The important factor is that there be no slowing down in the speed of the approach to the jump.

2. *Failure to use arms and legs adequately.* Many girls have not learned to use the total body to jump adequately. In order to use the arms in the upward lift they must be forcefully drawn back in the final stages of the approach. In order to use the legs in jumping they must be flexed during the approach and the center of gravity must be lowered into a deep crouch from the left foot stride into either the jump-to-two-feet or stride-close takeoffs. Often the player will take the running approach with the center of gravity relatively high and then attempt to crouch and jump in sequence after the two feet make contact. This action completely destroys the momentum developed in the approach and results in jumping too late. Corrections for these errors are to improve arm, shoulder, and leg flexibility and strength, followed by repeated practice and coaching on the appropriate approach and jump mechanics without attempting to hit a ball.

Lack of power and/or control.

1. *Closed fist.* Striking the ball with a closed fist results in poor control because of the small, uneven striking surface. It also results in lack of power because the wrist's range of movement is impeded by the tightness created by the clenched fist. The correction is to hit the ball with an open hand, leading with the heel of the hand and sending the fingers over the top of the ball as it is contacted. This should be practiced as an isolated pattern until the player feels comfortable doing it. The practice progression is given in the section at the end of this chapter.

2. *Cupped hand.* A cupped hand in which the fingers are slightly flexed and held tightly together is a poor striking surface for the same reason given under the closed fist above. Corrections are also the same as given above.

3. *Wrist not hyperextended.* Many girls and women with poor throwing patterns have difficulty spiking because they do not know what it feels like to hyperextend or cock the wrist. As a result they push at the ball with the wrist extended or slightly flexed. The resulting spike lacks power and is often illegally contacted. Correction may include the demonstration of a hyperextended hand position and practice hitting the ball diagonally forward into the floor from a stationary position (fig. 4.17).

4. *Frozen wrist.* Overcompensation for lack of hyperextension may result in freezing the wrist in the hyperextended position. The ball is, therefore, hit without top spin or great force. Correction may require an exaggerated request of the player: "try to follow through with your hand under your armpit." It will also be beneficial to have repeated practice in the practice progression for learning to contact the ball which is given at the end of this chapter.

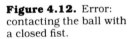

Figure 4.12. Error: contacting the ball with a closed fist.

Hitting ball too low (into net).

1. *Jumping too late.* This is usually a result of poor approach timing. It may be caused by the jump pattern described above in which a straight-legged run is followed by a delayed crouch to jump. It may be caused by the spiker failing to be in a ready position to start the approach. Even though the spiker must wait to approach, she should feel ready to start as a sprinter does in the starting blocks in track. The correction is to do isolated work on the approach technique, coaching for being "ready" and "driving hard" into the jump. The setter should set the ball slightly higher than usual to assist this player in having more time until she improves her approach.

2. *Too far from ball.* Again, this may be a result of poor approach timing as described in the late jump error above. If this is the case, correction procedures are identical. The player may, however, need to have the proper ball position explained again. She may have developed an improper concept of body and ball relationship. This would be followed by repeated practice to "get the feet to the ball."

3. *Failure to fully extend arm.* This may be the result of a poorly learned overhead throwing pattern transferred from softball or baseball. The most effective correction is to physically move the player's arm through the correct extension of the elbow so that full reach is felt, followed by repeated practice in the wall volley drill for spikers explained at the end of this chapter. This error may also be a result of a lazy habit of an experienced player. Practice spiking over a 7'6''-8' net will force the player into developing the correct feel of reaching fully.

Figure 4.13. Error: too far away from the ball.

Hitting ball long (out of bounds).

1. *Broad jumping.* This may result in a long hit if the broad jump carries the spiker's body under the ball. The ball is contacted at the bottom rather than at the back or top, as desired. Corrections are given under "Lack of body control in approach," on page 52.
2. *Approaching too soon.* If the player starts the approach early and goes into the jump without waiting for the ball, often the bottom back of the ball (fig. 4.14) will be struck rather than the back and top as desired. Corrections are given above under "Lack of height in the jump."
3. *Lack of wrist action.* The failure of the wrist to snap over the ball, thus creating top spin, may cause a spike in which all other factors are correct to go out of bounds in the backcourt. An analysis of the various aspects of this problem are given in the "Lack of Power and Control," on page 52.

Approach errors limiting ball placement.

1. *Starting approach inside court.* Beginners and some intermediates forget to move laterally outside the court in preparation for the spike. As a result a good set forces them to move toward the sideline away from the middle of the opponent's court. The spike which results is usually weak and often hit out of play over the sideline. Initial instruction should emphasize the out-of-court approach. Practice to encourage this might be done by placing a stationary player on the sideline about four feet from the net, forcing the spiker to move out and around her to make the approach.
2. *Side to net.* On-hand spikers frequently squarely face their setters as they approach the ball. As a result, the left shoulder and hip are sideways to the net (fig. 4.15), effectively screening out all down the line shots and forcing the ball cross court. Off-hand spikers guilty of facing the setter as they approach the ball also hit cross court and often out of bounds. This approach limits the range of shoulder rotation and backswing, leaving the armswing across the body as the only available source of power. Although the takeoff should be at a slight angle to the net rather than square to the net, frequently asking players who turn their shoulders too much to "try to get square to the net" as they take off produces the desired result. Having someone other than the spiker toss the ball to the setter in spiking drills may also help.
3. *Running past ball.* A player who runs past the ball either hits it off-center or turns and swings back across the body to hit it. Either way the ball can only be hit in one direction and usually goes out of bounds. The player must be given help in conceptualizing the correct alignment; this should be followed by much practice in getting the hitting shoulder directly behind the ball with hips relatively parallel to he net.

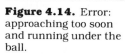

Figure 4.14. Error: approaching too soon and running under the ball.

Figure 4.15. Error: approaching ball with side toward net.

4. *Not moving laterally far enough to get behind the ball.* This error forces the spiker to reach laterally to strike the ball. The ball is usually contacted quite low and must travel in the direction the player is reaching. This correction usually must occur early in the approach. The intent must be to get the feet and body to the ball and *behind* the ball. On bad sets the lateral movement must be made before the final stride and jump occurs. Practice in getting to bad sets in good alignment will aid correction.

Effective spiking entails more than swinging at the ball and hoping it goes in. The spiker must consider both the placement of the set and the location of the defensive players and then decide what course to take. Some factors the spiker should consider are listed below.

Decisions Made by the Spiker

1. *Cross court.* When not sure where the block is or how the defense is aligned, hit the ball cross court. The ball probably will not go for a winner, but it may avoid the block. Since cross court is the strongest angle available, the ball will be hit hard enough to force the defense to be alert to pick it up.
2. *Close set.* When the setter puts the ball on top of the net and you are seemingly trapped by the block, consider the following alternatives:
   a. On the on-hand side, swing across the back of the ball from left to right with very little force, thereby brushing the ball off the hands of the middle blocker or bypassing her hands completely.

b. On-hand or off-hand, when sure the side blocker is going up, cut the ball toward the outside hand of the side blocker. Unless she takes her hands down as you turn on the ball, the ball will contact her hand and continue its flight out of play beyond the sideline.

c. Spike the ball up toward the top of the blocker's hands. If successful, the ball will contact the fingers and travel up and deep to the opponent's court.

d. Dink the ball over or around the block.

3. *Good set to side spiking position.* On a good set to one of the two sidelines the spiker should be in-balance and able to look at the opposing block. One of the following openings may be available to her:

a. *The line.* If the line is open and the spiker is sure of her alignment with the ball, she should hit through the opening down the line. However, if she is at all off-balance, she should go cross court.

b. *Between blockers.* If as she is in the air she sees that the middle blocker is a little late and an opening exists between the blockers, the ball should be hit between them.

c. *Block set wide.* If the block takes the line, aim for the middle of the court.

d. *One player block.* When it is obvious that the middle blocker is out of the play and you will be hitting against a one-player block, hit the ball cross court and sharply down.

e. *Short blocker.* Know who your blockers are. If one is extremely short, hit over her unless you are off balance and it is easier to hit the other direction. If one is extremely tall DO NOT try to go over her. Be alert to any exchanging of positions the blockers may make. The short girl down the line may have exchanged positions with the tall center front or vice versa.

Attack Variations

The Dink

When executed properly, the dink is an offensive technique in which a potential spiker contacts the ball on her fingers with only slight forward motion of the arm, sending the ball over or around the block and into the opponent's court (fig. 4.16).

Description of the dink technique. The technique for the dink is the same as the spike until the point at which the spiker is in the air and her arms are in front of her at shoulder height. At this point her spiking hand reaches up for the ball with the elbow, wrist, and fingers extended. The ball is contacted on the insides of the last joints of the fingers and released immediately without flexing the wrist or fingers.

If the ball is to be directed to the side rather than straight ahead, the wrist and fingers must be facing the direction of the dink at the time of contact. Any attempt to redirect the ball by turning the wrist or fingers will result in an illegal contact.

Figure 4.16. The dink.

If the spiker contacts the ball higher than the blocker's hands or is dinking away from the block, her release should be forward. If the ball must go over the block, she must contact the ball further underneath to send it up and forward.

The dink is most effective when placed immediately behind the blockers. Usually a dink to the ten foot line is easily handled because the defense has time to move to the ball.

Although the dink is useful in playing balls from an off-balanced position which would not likely produce a successful spike, this action is easily read by the defense. Most effective are dinks hit off of good sets forcing the defense to remain deep in case the ball is spiked. Several successful dinks will often force the defense to change its court positions opening up more of the court to the spike placements. However, if a player always dinks and never spikes, the defense will be waiting for it.

Common errors. Common errors on the dink include taking the ball too low, carrying the ball in the fingers and palm and flexing the wrist to direct the ball. All are illegal contacts of the ball. To correct these errors the player must concentrate on making contact with arm and wrist at full extension.

Off-speed Spike

A hard-hit spike is not always the most effective. Many times when the defense is set for a hard spike, one hit at less than normal speed will catch them flat-footed. The technique for the off-speed spike is the same as for a regular spike until the hand starts forward to spike the ball. Its forward motion is reduced and the ball is contacted a little below center with a great deal of top spin. This enables the ball to clear the block and drop into the middle of the court.

1. Practice procedures should be organized so that all players are actively involved as much of the time as possible.
2. In most drills players should work in no more than twos, threes or fours. There should be enough balls so that one is available for every two players.
3. It is important to be aware of the pace of practice. Each player should receive adequate time for practice; rotate players on time, and move efficiently from one practice procedure to the next.
4. Players should know what the drill is for and be aware of the specific demands for relating it to a game situation.
5. Attempt to utilize the techniques practiced in a game situation relatively soon after isolated technique practice.
6. The coach should try to see each player perform, using cue words for assistance. If the group as a whole has a problem, re-explain to everyone. If one player has difficulty, arrange for individual work, but keep the team moving in purposeful practice while individual coaching takes place.

Practice Progressions

Purpose

Making Proper Contact with Ball

Description and Specifications

1. One player, one ball. Hold the ball chest high; hit ball out of hand to floor with heel of hand, followed with wrist snap, bringing hand over the ball. Concentrate on leading with the elbow, with the elbow held high. Pronate the wrist with contact.
2. Two players, one ball. Face the partner at distance of 15–18 feet. Toss ball short distance into air in front of hitting shoulder. Using hitting action as in #1 above, hit ball to floor to rebound up to partner. Concentrate on wrist snap and acquiring top spin.
3. One ball, one player. Facing a wall, toss and hit the ball to the floor just short of the wall. Ball will rebound upward off the wall. Player can catch the ball and repeat, or position and hit the rebouding ball for continuous volley (fig. 4.17).

Purpose	Description and Specifications

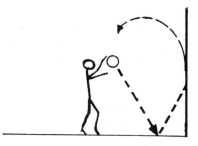

Figure 4.17. Wall spike.

4. Three or more players, three or more balls. Players line up on sidelines, with first player 3–4 feet from net. Each player in line has a ball. Tosser stands 1–2 feet from the net, 3–4 feet from the sideline. Players in line each in succession: toss ball to tosser who catches it; tosser lobs high pass in upward arc in front of player who attempts to position behind the ball and hit the ball over the net with top-spin without jumping; hitter recovers her own ball and goes to end of line.

Approach, Footwork

1. Large group. Space out in area. Coach turns back to group. Group follows coach in walking through footwork. Repeat until it can be done up to speed with proper slow-slow-quick timing, with jump.
2. Large group. Start at one end of gym. Eight or more squad lines. First in each line do repeated approaches in sequence across the entire floor.

Approach, Controlling Momentum

Large group. Space out so that 6–8 players are side by side on each side facing the net, at 10 foot line. Coach facing across

Purpose

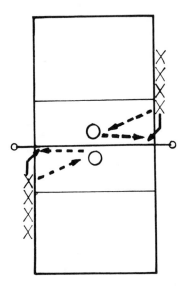

Figure 4.18. Basic spiking drill.

the net. On signal, spikers pass imaginary ball to a setter, turn to approach net and jump. Concentrate on arm lift, shoulder rotation, and landing with hips back, and weight on heels to convert forward momentum. This same drill can be done moving toward a wall.

Combine Approach and Hitting

The basic spike practice drill is shown in Figure 4.18. Spiking lines start outside the sidelines, 8–10 feet from the net. Each spiker has a ball. Spiker tosses or passes a pass to the setter who sets for spike. Set should be close for tall spikers and farther from the net for short spikers. Spikers should wait on approach until ball is off setter's hands. (If setters are not consistent, tossed sets can be used.) Spiker retrieves her own hit and goes to the end of the opposite line. Both on-hand and off-hand pactice are needed.

Purpose	**Description and Specifications**
Placement	After the basic technique has been learned players should attempt to place the ball at will to (a) the line, (b) long angle, (c) sharp cross court. A portion of each practice time must be spent on placement. The coach may call the angle as the player is in the end of her approach, and the player should hit that angle.
Variations	1. Have a tosser pass the ball to the setter. This is more realistic to the game for the spiker.
	2. Place two spiking lines, one on either side of the court. The setter chooses the spiker. The spiker not should practice coming off for the cover of the other spiker.
	3. Practice the center hit with setter offset to right of center.
	4. Practice multiple offense with setter offset to right of center. Three spiking lines. Center front passes ball to setter. Setter chooses set. Any combination of choices can be isolated with two lines, LF and CF, CF and RF, etc.
Spiking with a Block	1. *One blocker up.* Start spike drill with blocker in position. As each spiker hits, she becomes the next blocker. Blocker retrieves the ball and goes to end of spiking line.
	2. *Two blockers up.* Two blockers take position at side and center starting positions. With set, center blocker moves to form block. Spiker attempts to read block and place ball. Rotation is spiker to side blocker, side

Purpose	Description and Specifications
	blocker to center blocker, center blocker retrieves and goes to spike line.
	3. *The over set.* With spiker, blocker, and setter. Setter chooses good set or over set. Spiker must make decision to hit, use block, or to put up a block. If ball is far enough over net, blocker may spike it.
Endurance	A tosser at backcourt is supplied with 8–10 balls. Retrievers and helpers assist to replenish supply. Tosser repeatedly tosses to setter who sets to the same spiker 10–20 times in succession. Spiker must hit, recover, back away from the net, and repeat the spike. This is excellent for teaching the reaction required of the spiker; that is, back away from the net to be ready to spike.
Spiking Bad Sets	Regular spiking lines, no setter. Coach tosses sets away from the net, outside the court, toward the middle of the court, etc. It is the objective of the player to (a) get the ball over the net, in court, (b) use an attacking hit if possible, (c) move to get as squarely behind the ball as possible.
Combinations	1. *Receive serve and spike.* Three players, one ball. 1 serves over the net to 2, 2 passes to 3, 3 sets for 2 as she adjusts approach to the pass and the potential angle for the set. Two groups can share a court with serve going opposite directions.

Purpose	Description and Specifications
	2. *Block then spike.* Six players, many balls. One spiker on each side directly opposite each other, one setter on each side, one tosser (CB) on each side. Tosser on one side passes, spiker hits, opposite spiker and setter block. As soon as setter on other side recovers the side, tosser passes a ball to the setter, and original blocker spikes as original spiker and setter block. Care must be taken to keep loose balls from under foot.
Recover from Defensive Save to Spike	Regular spiking line with backcourt tosser and setter. Spiker executes a lunge and shoulder roll; as shoulder roll is being completed, tosser passes to setter; setter sets to player who did roll, who must recover, get up, approach and spike.
Dink Variation	1. Regular spike lines with setter. Place a rope 10–15 inches higher than the net. Place towels on the floor to indicate point of aim. Take spike approach and dink over the rope to spot.
	2. Same as above, eliminating rope and place two-player block in position. Towels may be used for aim, but blockers should be aware of them and avoid backing up (towels may cause slip and fall).

5

The Block

The block is the first line of defense against a spike. It is executed by one or more players close to the net who jump into the air and place their hands in line with the anticipated flight of the spike. By so doing, they hope to slow down the spike or prevent it from coming onto their side of the net.

Basic Technique

General Description

Ready position. All three front-row players are eligible to block. Therefore, they should maintain the blocking ready position as long as the ball is on the opponent's side of the net and is capable of being spiked across the part of the net for which they are responsible.

In the ready position the feet are in a side-stride position, shoulder width apart. The knees are easy and the weight slightly forward. The hands are held open, fingers extended and spred, to form a surface parallel to the net. The elbows point down and away from the body, placing the hands slightly outside the shoulders at about shoulder height and six inches closer to the net than the rest of the body.

Figure 5.1. Movement of middle blocker to form a double block.

Movement to the ball. When a single block is utilized the blocker should move to a position in line with the power spike in one lateral sliding step. In a double block at the sideline the middle blocker must move laterally to a position next to the side blocker. In a center block the side blocker must move to close off the area next to the position established by the middle blocker. Since this necessitates covering almost half the width of the court in a relatively short amount of time the movement must be rapid.

Footwork for a middle blocker moving to her left (fig. 5.1) is initiated by a slide step with the left foot (frame 1), followed by a long crossover step with the right foot (frame 2). Upon landing the blocker pivots on the right foot to face the net as she places her left foot firmly next to the outside blocker's right foot (frame 3). The left foot is planted slightly inward on the final step to enable the blocker to transfer her momentum vertically rather than laterally.

The armswing in the crossover step is similar to the movement of the arms for the spike approach. The middle blocker's hand nearest the center of the court is extended behind her prior to the final pivot (frame 2). As she pivots and her side-stride position is established, the arms are brought up to a position in which the forearms are parallel to the net. At the completion of the third step the feet are shoulder-width apart, the body and forearms are parallel to the net and the hands are approximately face high. Throughout these movements both players must be watching the ball and the approaching spiker. Through peripheral vision the middle blocker must also know the location of the side blocker in order to be able to judge the length of her final step. It is the responsibility of the end blocker to set the block against the outside attack.

The jump. To initiate the jump, the feet are planted square to the net and are in a slightly toed-in position. The blocker flexes her knees at an angle which yields her the greatest vertical lift. As the blocker explodes upward her arms extend and the hands and forearms penetrate the plane of the net.

Figure 5.2. Position of blocker's hands in the ATTACK BLOCK.

Figure 5.3. Position of blocker's hands in the SOFT BLOCK.

The blocker should time her jump so that she is at the peak of her jump or just beginning her descent as the spiker contacts the ball. On a normal set the blocker jumps shortly after the spiker jumps. The delayed jump is necessary because the spiker's approach and arm swing enable her to jump higher than the blocker; if the blockers went up with the spiker, they would be on their way down as the ball is contacted. Against a low, quick set where the spiker jumps before the ball is set, the blocker must jump with the spiker.

Short or poor jumping blockers may have difficulty placing their hands above the net. They should attempt to jump from a full squat position. If more height is needed they must start 2–3 feet back from the net, step forward, and swing the arms toward the net and up. This will give more height, but the likelihood of netting with the hands, being too far from the net, mistiming the jump, or broad-jumping, are greatly increased. Therefore, the technique of starting the block from back off the net would be used only by very poor jumpers or short blockers.

Hand position and contact with the ball. In the ATTACK BLOCK (fig. 5.2), the blocker reaches straight up from the shoulders to a fully extended position in which the hands and forearms penetrate the plane of the net. The back is slightly hunched and the eyes focus on the spiker. The wrists are tilted forward with the fingers rigid and spread wide. The thumbs are approximately one to two inches apart. The ball is contacted with the palm of the hand as the wrists are snapped forward. The purpose of the attack block is to intercept the flight of the ball before it crosses the net.

In the SOFT BLOCK (fig. 5.3), the hand position varies from the attack block in that the forearms are held parallel to the net, while the hands are

parallel to the net or tilted slightly backward. The soft block is commonly used to block balls set off the net and by shorter blockers who can cover a greater area above the net by using the soft blocking technique.

When blocking at the sideline, the outside blocker should turn her hand nearest the sideline in toward the middle of the opponent's court. The practice prevents the spiker from brushing the ball off the blocker's hand toward the sideline.

Follow-through. After contacting the ball the blocker withdraws her hands and arms away from the net and to her side to avoid a net violation. Upon contact with the floor the blocker's knees flex to absorb the force of the landing.

This section identifies the common errors in individual and team blocking. No attempt is made to state a specific correction for each error since it is the same for all errors: identification of the problem, positive cuing, and practice to correct it. The section at the end of this chapter on practice progressions should aid in structuring practice for improving performance.

Common Errors— Identification

Jumping too soon. Blockers who jump at the same time as the spiker find themselves on the way down while the spiker is at the top of her jump.

Swinging arms forward. Blockers who swing the arms forward and up often commit net fouls (fig. 5.4). Forearms should remain parallel with the net until the elbows are shoulder height.

Figure 5.5. Error:
arms extended in line
with ears.

Figure 5.6. Error:
hands too far apart.

Arms in line with ears. Players who block by extending the arms up in line with their ears have little power and cannot block aggressively. They also frequently net with some other part of their body if their hands are close to the net. If their hands are back from the net to avoid a net foul, the ball can usually be hit between their hands and the net. The arms are to be placed diagonally forward from the shoulder with wrists 3 to 4 inches from the net.

Closing eyes as spiker swings. Blockers who never adjust in their direction of the ball as the spiker starts to swing frequently have their eyes closed.

Fingers held together. Some players block with their fingers extended, but hold them together, possibly out of fear of injury (fig. 5.6). This greatly reduces the area covered by the block. Fingers should be spread, firm, and parallel with the net. Injuries to fingers held in this position are extremely rare.

Hands apart. A spiked ball can pass between the hands of a blocker whose thumbs are more than two inches apart (fig. 5.6). A player who blocks with hands shoulder width apart or who reaches laterally for a ball with one hand is inviting the spiker to hit the ball between her hands.

Double Block—not together. If the closing player is late starting, slow moving, or the set is very low, she will often have to jump before she is next to her blocking partner. If she goes straight up from this position an opening is created between the hands of the two blockers, usually in line with the spiker's power hit. About all the late blocker can do is reach laterally toward her partner making sure both hands are parallel with the net. The last factor is extremely important. If the late blocker blocks in the direction she is most likely facing, the ball can be hit between the two blockers.

Double block—closing player jumping laterally. The closing blocker must be certain that the foot closest to her blocking partner is firmly planted, and that she pushes strongly with it as she jumps up to bring her center of gravity inside her base of support. Otherwise, she will tend to jump laterally into her blocking partner, a practice resulting in a high incidence of injury.

Suggested Practice Procedures for the Block

Preparation and Use

1. Practice procedures should be organized so that all players are actively involved as much of the time as possible.
2. In most drills players should work in no more than twos, threes, or fours. There should be enough balls so that one is available to every two players.
3. It is important to be aware of the pace of practice. Each player should receive adequate time for practice; rotate players on time, and move efficiently from one practice procedure to the next.
4. Players should know what the drill is for and be aware of the specific demands for relating it to a game situation.
5. Attempt to utilize the techniques practiced in a game situation relatively soon after isolated technique practice.
6. The coach should try to see each player perform, using cue words for assistance. If the group as a whole has a problem, re-explain to everyone. If one player has difficulty, arrange for individual work, but keep the team moving in purposeful practice while individual coaching takes place.

Practice Progressions

Purpose	Description and Specifications
Basic Technique	Large group. Arrange players arms distance apart the width of the net for each court in use. Players face the net with toes about 18 inches from center line. Coach is opposite facing all courts. On signal, players lower body and jump, working on proper mechanics of block.

Purpose	Description and Specifications
Lateral Movement	Large group, towels draped over net at sidelines and at center. A line is formed on each side of the net at one side of the court. First two players face one another in good blocking ready position. On signal, both turn and move laterally to execute a block over each towel to the far sideline. Each set of players in turn do the same. When lines are completed, the movement is made back in the opposite direction. Concentration is on balance, footwork, control, and jumping.
Forming the Double Block	Large group. Form four squad lines per court, one at each sideline, two side by side at the center of the court. The first player in each line facing the net is 3–4 feet from the net. On signal, first player in each line moves to a ready position at the net to prepare for a block. On a second signal the two center blockers move laterally to their respective sides and locate the side blocker. On signal the two blockers jump together. Once coordination is assumed, change signals to "ready" and "go." As soon as the center blocker reaches side blocker, they jump together.
Blocking a Spiker	1. *One blocker.* Start a spiking drill with a blocker in position. As each spiker hits, she becomes the next blocker. The blocker retrieves the ball and goes to the end of the spiking line.

Purpose	Description and Specifications
	2. *Two blockers.* Start a spiking drill with blockers taking position at sideline and at center. With set, center blocker moves to form block.
Center Blocker Waits for Set	Place blockers in each position. Start spiking drill with a setter and spiking lines for both on-hand and off-hand. Backcourt toss to setter. Setter chooses front or backset. Center blocker tries to "read" setter to anticipate set. If setter is deceptive, center blocker must hold. Blocker away from set should practice moving away from the net to simulate a real game situation.
Taking the Angle, Taking the Line	In any of the drills above, the blockers should predetermine whether the line or the power angle will be taken away from the spiker. They should work hard to coordinate this appropriately.
Blocking Against the Multiple Offense	Three blockers are placed in ready position. Three spiking lines with the off-center right setter are established across the net. CF passes to the setter who chooses the appropriate spiker. The setter may vary height as well as direction of set. The center blocker must hold until the ball is set. She should work to read the setter; if deceptive, blockers must block one on one. If the setter gives a clue to the center set, the appropriate side blocker should move to form a double block toward the center.

6

Individual Defense

Although individual defense is played within the context of a team defensive system, individual defensive efforts contribute dramatically to the challenge and excitement of the game. Backcourt defense is essentially a reaction skill which not only requires physical technique, but also anticipation, concentration and determination.

Basic Technique

General Description

Ready position. The basic ready position is a semisquat with the feet in a front-back stride position and spread wider than shoulder width; weight forward on the inside balls of the feet; arms in front of body; elbows easy with hands separated and held waist high.

When the forearm pass is utilized for the purpose of recovering a hard spiked ball it is referred to as a dig. The fundamental techniques of the forearm pass need to be incorporated into backcourt defensive skills as the dig is an extension of the forearm pass. Basic technique for the forearm pass is included in

Chapter 2. At the time the opposing spiker contacts the ball the digger should stabilize her body with a short hop forward to a two foot landing which will place her in a position of readiness to react to the hit.

Figure 6.1. Dig and half roll.

Passing a Hard Spiked Ball

The skill of digging requires the player to cushion the ball by utilizing one of the following techniques:

(1) The player can absorb the ball force by falling backwards from a low crouch position as she contacts the ball (fig. 6.1).

The player moves to a position in line with the ball, facing the passing target. Additionally, the player should contact the ball from a deeply crouched position, passing the ball at approximately knee height. As long as the ball is in contact with the arms they must be at the desired angle to the pass, although the player's weight should be moving backward as the ball is contacted (fig. 6.1, frame 2). The followthrough consists of a backward fall, landing first on the buttocks on the side of the rear foot (frame 3), and then rolling onto a curled lower back (frame 4). The hands come apart after the ball has been passed and follow the body momentum backward. Once the backward momentum is diminished the player snaps legs and arms forward to bring her back to her feet.

(2) The player may drop the arms straight back on contact of the ball to absorb the force of the hit (fig. 6.2).

The player moves to a position in line with the ball, facing the passed target. The player should contact the ball from a low body position with the feet spread wider than shoulder width, and weight forward on the inside balls of the feet. As the ball contacts the forearms the arms are straight and drop back toward the passer in the follow-through (fig. 6.2, frame 3).

To extend the player's court coverage for defensive recoveries the roll and dive are defensive techniques that can be utilized.

The Dig and Roll

Even players with superior agility and anticipation cannot move fast enough to pass all balls from a balanced position. Rather than letting the ball go because it is too far in front, behind, or to the side to be reached from a standing

Figure 6.2. Straight
arm pull back.

or crouched position, the superior player extends her court coverage by making
a low extended lunge for a forearm pass. She follows this with a shoulder roll
to protect her in the fall and to allow recovery for the next play. The roll can
be combined with the forearm pass to reach a spiked ball or a ball with minimal velocity falling far from the passer.

Dig and roll—hard spiked ball (fig. 6.3). When executing the roll to recover
from digging a hard spiked ball the player has time to take only one step with
the lunging foot in the direction of the ball. As her body weight is shifted over
this leading foot the knee flexes deeply to receive the weight. If the ball is in
line with or inside the passer's leading knee it can be passed with a two-arm
dig. However, if it is outside the player's knee she must reach with the arm
nearest the ball and execute a one-arm dig. This is done by getting any part
of the forearm to the ball at an angle that will get the ball up.

Figure 6.3. Dig and
roll.

In both instances, as soon as the ball has been contacted the player executes a backward pivot on the foot of the leading leg and her lateral momentum pulls her over onto the floor. On the two-arm dig she lands on her buttocks, while in the one-arm dig she lands on the side of the thigh and buttocks. From either of these positions the player has sufficient lateral momentum to carry her onto her back into a shoulder roll and an upright landing on both feet.

The player should not think about the roll until the ball has been passed. However, by that time she should have lowered her weight and started her pivot, ready to lower her buttocks to the floor. This can be seen in frame 2 of Figure 6.3. As the buttocks contact the floor she should concentrate on rolling her weight diagonally across her back toward the shoulder opposite the pivot foot, and then attempt to bring both knees across that shoulder. Both knees should be tucked to start the roll. As the knees start over the shoulder, the knee on the same side as the rolling shoulder should remain tucked, while the other knee should extend and reach back for the floor. This brings the player's weight to a supporting position on the tucked knee and ball of the reaching foot, with arms ready to help push the player to her feet, if necessary. This sequence can be seen in frames 3–6 of Figure 6.3.

Players usually find it easier to roll toward the side of their dominant hand. Therefore, the coach must be alert to set up practice situations requiring rolls in both directions. The basic roll technique should be learned on a mat, and then on the floor, coupled with a pass.

The dig and roll are also used to field a ball in front or to the rear of a player. Executing the roll to the rear is difficult only because it is hard to follow the ball. The forward movement to the dig and roll is much simpler, although the passer must remember to pivot before the ball is passed so that her side and arms, rather than her knees and front side, contact the floor.

When executing the dig and roll diagonally forward a player must remember to use the foot nearest the ball as the lead foot, even though it might

Figure 6.4. Front dig and roll.

be possible to reach the ball by stepping across her body with the foot furthest from the ball. For example, a player attempting to pass a ball well in front to her left should lunge for the ball with her left foot leading and pivot backwards on the left foot so that she rolls onto her back and across her right shoulder. This places the contact point with the ball between her body and the target. Many players attempt the same pass lunging with their right leg and pivoting to the rear, resulting in a roll across their left shoulder. This latter technique places the passer's body between the contact point with the ball and the target. From this position is it very difficult to angle the forearms toward the net; as a result the ball is frequently passed backwards, away from the net and out of play.

Dig and roll—nonspiked ball (fig. 6.4). The roll can also be used in conjunction with the forearm pass when attempting to cover a great distance in pursuit of a dink, teammate's mispassed ball or a ball dropping off a block or the net. The main difference in the roll on this recovery play is that it is faster because of the greater body momentum built up running to the ball. The technique is the same as when passing a hard spike and rolling except that force needs to be added rather than taken away from the pass. This is accomplished by swinging the passing arm or arms up to contact the ball (frames 2 and 3).

Pass and roll common errors—causes and corrections.

1. *Falling on the knee.* Failing to pivot on the lead foot results in a body part other than the buttocks, usually the knee (fig. 6.5) absorbing the body's weight as it contacts the floor. Injury frequently results and the roll is often incomplete. Isolated practice of the lunge and pivot should be done. The weight should be on the ball of the foot; contact on the heel will slow down the pivot.
2. *Hard falls.* When a player attempts to contact the ball as high off the floor as possible by jumping laterally to contact it injury often results due

to the distance of the fall. This practice also results in a weak pass because the body is falling away from the direction of the pass. Players must learn to let the ball drop lower. Concentrate on starting low and making all movement as low and parallel to the floor as possible.

3. *Starting the roll too early.* Players who lunge for the ball too soon are forced to pivot and contact the floor before the ball is passed. As a result the roll must be inhibited in order to wait for the ball to drop. The player feels pinned to the floor with no momentum available to help her add force to her pass. Players who start too early and go ahead with the roll before the ball leaves their arms have no success with their pass, although they may roll beautifully. Players and coaches alike must remember that the pass and roll should be judged by the success of the pass, not the gracefulness of the roll.

4. *Roll over wrong shoulder.* Beginners and some intermediate players attempt to roll over the shoulder on the same side of the body as the lead leg. This results in an inhibition of momentum and a slower or incomplete roll. It sometimes results in injury to the neck when the body weight is borne there. Time should be taken to break down the technique and then by much isolated practice of the roll on a mat.

Figure 6.5. Error: failure to pivot, resulting in landing on knee.

Figure 6.6. Dig and dive.

5. *Side roll.* Some beginners roll by taking a lateral step and a fall, landing simultaneously on the hip, elbow, and shoulder. From this position they roll sidewards across the backbone to an upright position on the opposite side. This technique shortens lateral range of movement and may result in bruising the sides of the knees, shoulders, and elbows.

The Dig and Dive

The dig and dive, illustrated in Figure 6.6, is another defensive technique designed to extend the range for possible defensive recoveries. Men tend to use the dive more than women because of their increased capacity for upper body strength. Although women may be capable of diving, the majority may find the front roll more efficient in terms of control and quicker recovery. The coach and player should work together in determining the defensive techniques best suited for the player.

The dive consists of a forward thrust of the entire body through the air in a horizontal position. It is initiated from a low body position as the digger extends forward to the ball. The back leg is kicked up and back which tips the body into a horizontal position from which the ball is passed. As the trailing leg is lifted the back is arched. The hands are spread as the arms are extended forward at approximately a 45 degree angle to the floor. Upon contact with the floor the digger pushes against the floor and slides forward on the chest and stomach to cushion the dive.

Dig and dive common errors—causes and correction.

1. *Split chin.* Failing to arch the back and lift the head can result in a split chin. Concentrate on lifting the head as the body slides forward to cushion the dive.
2. *Hard falls.* Diving from a high position can result in a hard landing. Concentrate on starting low and making all movements as low and parallel to the floor as possible. The digger should push the body forward with her hands to cushion the dive.

1. Practice procedures should be organized so that all players are actively involved as much of the time as possible.
2. In most drills players should work in no more than twos, threes or fours. There should be enough balls so that one is available for every two players.
3. It is important to be aware of the pace of practice. Each player should receive adequate time for practice; rotate players on time, and move efficiently from one practice procedure to the next.
4. Players should know what the drill is for and be aware of the specific demands for relating it to a game situation.
5. Attempt to utilize the techniques practiced in a game situation relatively soon after isolated technique practice.
6. The coach should try to see each player perform, using cue words for assistance. If the group as a whole has a problem, re-explain to everyone. If one player has difficulty, arrange for individual work, but keep the team moving in purposeful practice while individual coaching takes place.

Suggested Practice Procedures for Individual Defense

Preparation and Use

Practice Progressions

Purpose
Reaction to Speed of Ball Flight

Description and Specifications
1. Two players, one ball. To build reaction to ball speed. Partner progressively increases speed and lowers trajectory of toss lob, basketball chest pass, sharp angle basketball two-hand overhead pass, one-hand volleyball hit. Tosses (hit) aimed at forearm passer's knees from about 15 feet. Concentrate on getting ball up and accurately back to tosser.

Purpose	Description and Specifications
	2. Four players, ten balls. Coach spikes balls repeatedly to digger in assigned position who digs balls to midcourt until the desired goal is achieved. The difficulty of the spikes can be controlled by the coach. Extra players shag balls and assist the coach.
Reaction to Speed of Flight and Lateral Movement	1. Two players, one ball. Combine with lateral movement to squarely face target (partner). Partner places ball 2–3 feet to either side.
	2. Combine with lateral movement and shoulder roll. Partner places ball 4–5 feet to either side. Concentrate on low starting position and low movement to ball, parallel to floor.
Developing Courage and Endurance	1. Coach and one player at a time, many balls, retriever and helper. Concentrate on consecutive hits and soft tosses placed to either side or in front of player. Execute forearm pass and roll and be ready to play next ball. Object is to get to each ball with the best technique possible and be ready for next play. Timed, progressive 15, 30, 45, 60 seconds.
	2. Four players, ten balls. Coach spikes balls repeatedly to digger in assigned position who digs, dives and rolls until fatigued. The players time is recorded. Extra players shag balls and assist coach.

Purpose

Combination with Other
Techniques

Description and Specifications

1. Pepper—(pass-set-spike) One
   ball, two players. 1 sets to 2; 2
   hits (spike type) to 1; 1 forearm
   passes to 2; 2 sets to 1; 1 hits to
   2, etc.
2. Receive serve and spike. One
   ball, 3 players. 1 serves to 2; 2
   passes to 3; 3 sets to 2 who
   spikes. Takes full court length
   and one-half court width. Passer
   who spikes works on adjusting
   her approach to her own pass to
   setter and setter's angle of set.
3. All spiking drills in later
   chapters can be adapted to
   include putting a player into
   position to try to read spiker
   and move to pick up the hit.

7

The Serve

The ball is put in play by a serve. It is a key offensive technique which can result in direct points or force the opponents into a defensive position.

Although it is possible to serve the ball underhand with considerable accuracy, the trajectory and lack of force in this technique makes it a defensive serve at all but beginning levels of play. A sidearm serve is also possible but lacks accuracy.

The overhand serve (fig. 7.1) can be a strong offensive weapon. It can be hit with a great deal of accuracy, and its trajectory and lateral movement can be altered by controlling the ball's spin.

The two overhand serves to be considered are the floater serve and the top-spin serve. All descriptions in this chapter refer to the movement for the right handed server.

Figure 7.1. The overhand serve (floater).

Ready Position. The ready position for both serves is the same. The server stands behind the legal serving area behind the baseline with her hips and shoulders square to the net. The ball is held at chest height in line with the right shoulder and right foot.

The feet are in a front-back stride position, with the left foot pointing toward the net, several inches ahead of the right. The right foot points diagonally toward the right sideline and supports the body weight.

Toss. The ball is tossed two to three feet in the air in front of the right shoulder. The ball is released at shoulder height although the left hand continues upward and forward.

If a floater serve is to be attempted with the valve stem in a preferred position upon contact, it is important that the upward force be applied through the center of the ball to avoid spinning.

Basic Technique

General Description

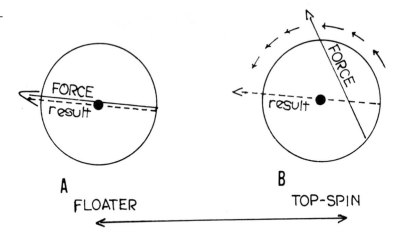

Figure 7.2. Force application and resulting trajectory on overhand serves.

A FLOATER

B TOP-SPIN

As the upward lift of the ball begins, the server concentrates most of the weight onto her right foot. As soon as the toss is released her right shoulder rotates, pulling her striking arm back, elbow flexed, hand opened, with wrist in easy hyperextension.

Forward swing. As the ball approaches the top of the toss a step is taken forward on the left foot. As the ball starts to drop forward rotation of the right hip and shoulder begins. The left hand drops as the right elbow leads the arm upward and forward. When the hips and shoulders are square to the net and the right upper arm almost parallel to the net, the elbow extends and the hand approaches the ball.

Contact: Floater serve. The floater serve, shown in Figure 7.2, is contacted slightly below the back of the ball with the heel of the hand. Upon contact and follow-through the wrist remains in easy hyperextension, thereby applying force forward and slightly upward through the center of gravity of the ball (fig. 7.2A). The ball is contacted with the elbow in full extension two to three inches in front of the server.

Contact: Top-spin serve. The ball is tossed slightly closer to the player for the top-spin serve. This enables her to contact the ball below the lower rear quadrant with the heel of the hand and hit it forcefully upward and forward (fig. 7.2B). As the wrist approaches the ball it is actively hyperextended and the elbow fully extended. Upon contact the wrist snaps forcefully up and forward, bringing the fingers up the back of the ball and over the top. See Figure 4.9 in the spiking description for an illustration of this.

Follow-through: Floater serve. To the player it feels like there is no follow-through on the floater serve because the wrist remains in easy hyperextension, stopping the hand from following the ball.

However, as shown in Figure 7.1, frame 6, the arm does follow through slightly toward the net with the body weight on the front foot.

Follow-through: Top-spin serve. The follow-through on the top-spin serve results in the wrist flexing and the hand and arm forcefully following the ball, much like the follow-through on a down-the-line spike (fig. 4.5). The weight is forward on the left leg.

Characteristics of the floater serve. The floater serve is most commonly used due to its greater accuracy and variety in flight pattern.

Analysis of Performance Factors

Because the arm swing is slower on the floater serve there is more time to make adjusting movements for insured accuracy. However, the main reason for the effectiveness of this serve is that it can be hit with no spin. Without the stabilizing action of spin, the ball is free to be acted upon by any other existing influences such as air currents or imbalances in the ball. As a result, the ball "floats" in unpredictable directions, making it difficult for the passer to receive the serve. Floater serves break to the left or right of their initial flight path, as well as dropping below or raising above their anticipated trajectory, as a result of the placement of the valve stem upon contact.

Characteristics of the top-spin serve. The top-spin serve travels in a laterally stabilized path, although it does drop sooner than a ball hit with the same initial trajectory but without spin. Because it drops rapidly it can be hit with a great deal of force and still drop into the opponent's court. The server may contact the ball in the lower right or left quadrant which will cause the ball to curve in flight.

Offensive serving includes more than hitting the serve hard or making it float. Strategic placement of the serve is most important. Good serving strategy includes the following:

Service Placement Strategy

1. Serve away from the strong spiker. This forces the setter to back set or run around the ball to set her.
2. Serve to any player known to be a weak passer. This will force her teammates to adjust their positions to cover for her, creating openings elsewhere in the court.
3. Serve many times at shoulder level of the front row players.
4. Attempt difficult short serves or corner serves only when you know your control is good.
5. Serve to a substitute who has just entered the game. She may be cold or a weak player.
6. Vary your serving pattern. If several short serves drop for winners don't press your luck. Serve deep; the opponents may still be worried about the shot serve and be caught by surprise.

7. On a multiple offense occasionally attempt to serve the ball into the path of the setter coming in from the backcourt.
8. On a multiple offensive send many serves down the line. This makes it difficult for the center spiker to follow the flight of the pass while getting into position to spike.

Common Errors—
Cause and
Correction

Lack of control.

1. *Failure to take a step into the serve.* This causes all of the force to be produced by arm and shoulder action. The stronger action of the weight shift and body turn has been eliminated. Concentrate on the forward-back stride, keeping the weight on the back foot until all the body parts begin to move forward in sequential action: step, body turn, and arm swing.
2. *Failure to take adequate backswing.* If the shoulders continue to face the net squarely after the toss inadequate momentum would be existent to send the ball over the net. The correction can be made by concentrating on rotating the right foot to the right and lifting the left hand forward and up with the toss as the back arches.
3. *Stepping into the serve too early.* Often a player will lose power by taking the forward step with the left foot as the ball is being tossed. The left foot may be placed forward with the toss, but the weight should not be transferred to this foot until the entire body is ready to rotate forward. Even though the body parts move in sequence, the player may feel the action if coached to "step with the arm swing."

Figure 7.3. Error: feet in side stride.

Figure 7.4. Error: punching at ball.

4. *Failure to extend the arm fully.* At contact the arm should be fully extended. Failure to do so will cause a punching action that may result in accuracy problems as well as lack of power. Correction may be made by concentrating on a higher toss and coaching the player to reach as high as possible.

Lack of accuracy—ball toss. Corrections for this entire section consist of practice on a ball toss just higher than a full reach over head with the ball just in front of the hitting arm after weight shift.

1. *Toss too low.* The ball will be hit into the net.
2. *Toss too far right.* The ball may be hit off-center to the right and out of bounds. If the arm swings out to the right to compensate for the toss the ball is hit weakly.
3. *Toss too far left.* The ball will usually be hit to the left. If the arm drops to compensate for the toss the ball may be hit weakly over the net or to the right.
4. *Toss too far forward.* Ball may be hit into the net. If a compensation is made by reaching forward and under the ball, it will be hit weakly in a high arc.
5. *Toss too far back.* Ball will travel in a high arc. This will usually be an extremely weak serve.

Figure 7.5. Error: tossing ball to far forward.

Figure 7.6. Error: ball tossed to far back.

Figure 7.7. Error: side to the net.

Lack of Accuracy—Techniques.

1. *Sidearm pattern.* Players who normally throw sidearm may tend to transfer this to the serve resulting in a ball that travels from right to left. The correction may be made by practicing the wall volley spiking drill (p. 58) on a line marked on the floor.
2. *Side to the net.* If the player starts the serve with the left side to the net, her only path of arm swing is relatively sidearm. The ball will travel in a right to left path. Work to have player start by facing the net with a forward-back stride stance.

Suggested Practice Procedures for the Serve

Preparation and Use

1. Practice procedures should be organized so that all players are actively involved as much of the time as possible.
2. In most drills players should work in no more than twos, threes, or fours. There should be enough balls so that one is available to every two players.
3. It is important to be aware of the pace of practice. Each player should receive adequate time for practice; rotate players on time, and move efficiently from one practice procedure to the next.
4. Players should know what the drill is for and be aware of the specific demands for relating it to a game situation.
5. Attempt to utilize the techniques practiced in a game situation relatively soon after isolated technique practice.

6. The coach should try to see each player perform, using cue words for assistance. If the group as a whole has a problem, re-explain to everyone. If one player has difficulty, arrange for individual work, but keep the team moving in purposeful practice while individual coaching takes place.

Practice Progressions

Purpose
Basic Technique

Description and Specifications

1. Two players, one ball. Players face one another across net at 10 foot lines. Hit ball to partner using overhead hitting pattern (see p. 83 for drill progression). After each three serves, move back two steps. Aim ball to partner. As distance increases concentrate on increasing trunk rotation and weight transfer.

2. Large group, one ball to each two players. Space players the entire width of each backcourt line with a partner across the net. Serve to the partner who will, in turn, serve back. Concentrate on ball toss, trunk rotation and weight shift, and reaching arm to full extension.

Placement

Large group, one ball to each two players. Place a serving line at each 10 foot serving area. One person serves at a time. Extra players retrieve serves from other side of net. Place serve (a) down the line and deep; (b) cross-court, deep; (c) center-court, deep; (d) down the line and short; (e) cross court and short; (f) center court and short. These are all spots of vulnerability. The short serve should land in the front one-third of the court and clear the

Purpose	Description and Specifications
	net only by 3–4 feet. Ball retrievers should call or signal good or out to server on serves close to lines.
Serving to a Receiving Formation	1. Aim serve at open spaces. 2. Pick on one player and serve to her wherever she is. 3. Serve the switch on a multiple offense. 4. Serve deep over CB to force RB or LB to decide who will take or receive it.

Part Three

Team Tactical Skills

8

Offensive Systems

The primary purpose in organizing an offensive system in volleyball is to capitalize on the individual capabilities of the various members of the team. This is done to increase the probability that the pass-set-spike pattern of play, the basic attack, will occur as frequently and effectively as possible within the limits of the skill level of the players.

Factors in Selection of the Offense

In determining which offensive system to use for any given season the following should be considered. First, the personnel should be realistically evaluated to determine: (1) how consistently the players can perform the fundamentals of technique with precision; (2) the specific abilities and limitations of setters to be able to spike, and spikers to be able to set; and (3) the potential of all the players to learn offensive coordinations of varying complexities.

Secondly, the practice situation must be considered. To be able to coordinate any offense in competition, all movement variations must be learned in practice to such a high degree that game reaction will be automatic. This takes time. The more complex the system the more time it will take to practice and learn the coordination necessary.

A complex system may theoretically create more opportunities for attacking plays than one less involved. However, the use of the more complex system may result in fewer successful plays executed by a team which has not mastered the team coordination, or whose individual players have insufficient skill to execute the techniques with precision.

A final factor in the choice of systems requires an evaluation of the ability of the spikers to perform within the precision demands of the set placements in the various attacking plays used.

The most consistent pass-set-spike pattern utilizes a regular set at, or one to two feet inside, the sideline tape. Assuming the spiker begins her approach from outside the sideline, sets near the sideline enable the spiker to approach the ball with her weight moving toward her opponent's court. The main reason, however, for the side set is that it provides the spiker with the longest spiking angles available anywhere on the court. For example, if a player spiking from the left-front position hits the ball straight down the line, she has a hitting distance thirty feet long (the length of the court) available to her. If she were to hit the ball sharply cross court she would likewise have a minimum of thirty feet for a spiking distance, depending on how sharply the spike were angled. Most significantly, if she were to spike the ball in the direction of her greatest power, toward the left-back corner of her opponent's court, the spiking distance would be roughly forty-two feet. Therefore, by setting the ball to the sideline, the spiker is afforded a minimum spiking distance of thirty feet and a maximum distance of forty-two feet. In contrast, a set in the exact center of the court provides minimum distances for the spiker. If the ball is hit straight ahead thirty feet of cout is available. If the ball is hit toward either corner, the greatest distance, the spike could be increased to roughly thirty-three feet. If the ball is cut toward either sideline the distance diminishes rapidly to a minimum of fifteen feet. Therefore, a center set affords a minimum spiking distance of fifteen feet and a maximum of roughly thirty-three feet.

The figures given above suggest that at any level of skill the spiker will have a better chance of putting the ball in court if the set is toward the sideline, rather than toward the center of the court. Furthermore, it would seem reasonable to conclude that a player who cannot consistently keep her spikes in the court from the side position under game conditions (expected in the less complex systems), should not be asked to play under the multiple offense systems in which she is expected to spike from the center of the net.

As one considers the appropriateness of the following offensive systems for any given team, the above discussion, as well as the additional personnel requirements given for each system should be realistically considered.

Although numerous offensive systems are possible most are variations of four basic systems: the 4–2, 5–1, 6–0 or 6–2. The first numeral in each system

Figure 8.1. Key to symbols.

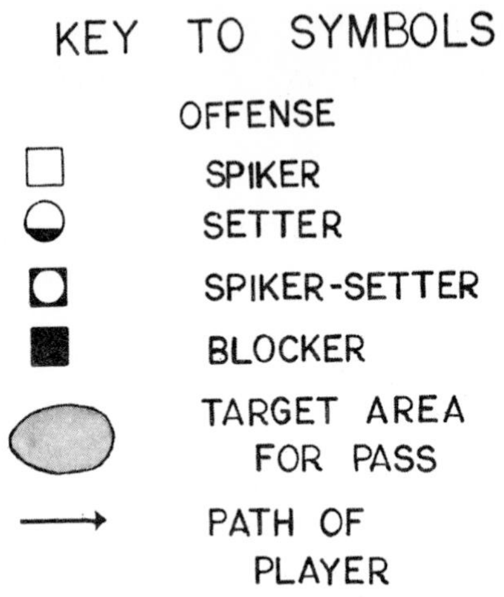

KEY TO SYMBOLS

OFFENSE

☐   SPIKER

◡   SETTER

▢   SPIKER-SETTER

◼   BLOCKER

⬭   TARGET AREA
               FOR PASS

⟶   PATH OF
               PLAYER

designates the number of spikers used; the second, the number of setters. Unless otherwise noted, all offensive systems described are based on the assumption that all players are right-handed.

The Four-Two Offense

The most frequently utilized offense is the four-two, or four spiker, two-setter system. Its advantages are its simplicity and personnel requirements. Four players must be able to spike, but should only occasionally be called upon to set. Two players do the majority of the setting and only occasionally are called upon to attack the ball. Thus, players are able to specialize in their strengths. However, if passing is poor, spikers may be forced to set and setters occasionally called upon to spike. The disadvantage of the 4–2 offense is that only two of the three front row players are used as spikers as the third is utilized to set the ball. This system of play is the one most commonly used with beginning levels.

Serve Reception

The first offensive play is initiated from the serve receiving position. In the 4–2 system the line-up is such that the two setters always have two spikers between them in the serving order. This insures the presence of one setter in the front row at all times. This can be seen in Figure 6.2A.

Four-two serve reception: Setter center front. In this formation (fig. 8.2) the setter is positioned close to the net, one to two feet to the right of the center of the net, facing the left front. In this position she is able to avoid receiving the serve, allowing her five teammates to pass the ball (contact #1), and leaving the setter available to set (contact #2) to either the left- or right-front spikers. Except when the serve is short and to the center of the court the setter moves back off of the net as soon as the serve passes the net. This saves steps once the ball has been passed since it places her more nearly in the center of the desirable passing zone.

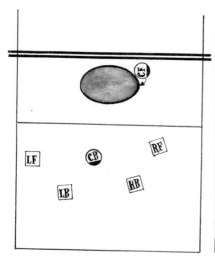

Figure 8.2. Four-two serve reception positions: setter center front.

It will be noted in Figures 8.2A and B that the entire receiving formation is offset to the left of the center of the court. This is done to take advantage of the restriction of the server to the right one-third of her court. In this situation, if the receiving team were equally distributed across the full width of the court, the right-front player would be in a position so that all balls to her right would be going out of bounds. It will also be seen that all of the receivers (except the setter) are deployed into the middle area of the court, when viewed from front to back. Since the ball must cross the net most serves will have a trajectory that will carry them at least to a depth of eight to ten feet from the net. The position shown will place the players in a position most advantageous to receive the serve.

Upon receiving the serve, the four spikers and the backcourt setter have the job of passing the ball to the center-front position. The left-front and right-front players assume the ready position in the approximate floor position indicated in Figure 8.2A. The center back moves forward to a position in line with the left- and right-front players in the center of the playing space between them. All three are responsible for serves waist high or below, in front or immediately to the right and left of them.

The left and right back are responsible for all serves higher than waist level for the front-court passers. Usually they are positioned so that any serves requiring more than one step backward to be passed with the forearms would be out of bounds. The left back stands in the middle of the space between the left front and the center back. She is responsible for serves in the backcourt area traveling between the left sideline and the left of the center-back's head. The right back takes serves passing over the area between the head of the center back and the right sideline. Both right- and left-back players should be prepared to back up the players in front of them, as well as one another.

Figure 8.3. Four-two serve reception positions: setter right front.

Four-two service reception: Setter right front. When the setter rotates one position to the right, the positions of all players, except the setter (right front) and the front row spiker closest to her (center front), remain essentially the same as when the setter was center front. Because it is desirable to have a spiker in the right front a switch is made between the right-front setter and the center-front spiker the instant the ball is served. This is done by positioning the center-front spiker at the right-front receiving position. Since the rules state that the right front (setter) must have all parts of her body more to the right of the court than the center front, she is placed next to the right sideline to avoid overlapping the center front. Again, the setter (right front) is close to the net to avoid having to pass the ball. The instant after the ball is contacted by the server the setter moves to the center front position, slightly away from the net, thus executing the switch. These players remain in switched positions until the next dead ball. They must realign according to serving order and the switch is repeated on each service from that position in rotation.

In this receiving position the switching spiker (center front) must not only avoid the left-right overlap with the setter (right front), but also prevent a front-back overlap with her corresponding backrow player (center back). Usually this front-back overlap is avoided by having the center back stand one step deeper in the court than the right front.

Four-two serve reception: Setter left front. When the setter rotates one position beyond right front she becomes a backrow player and thus a passer upon receiving the serve. The second setter in the four-two system is now in the left front and takes over the setting duties. Prior to the ball being served she stands next to the left sideline and close to the net (fig. 8.4B). The spiker nearest the setter (the center front) moves to a receiving position along the left sideline, being careful not to create a left-right overlap with the left front (the setter)

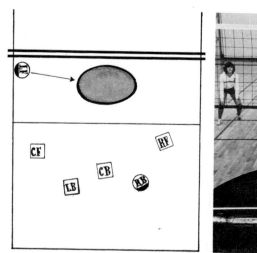

or a front-back overlap with the center back. As soon as the ball is served the setter (left front) moves to the center of the net, three to four feet away from it.

Figure 8.4. Four-two serve reception positions: setter left front.

Four-two Switch when Serving

When the setters are at either the right-front or left-front positions, the switch with the center forward is greatly simplified for the serving team. The two switching players position halfway between their respective areas. Since the ball must be received and returned by the opponents before the offense will begin to function, players simply take positions near one another, being careful not to overlap positions or screen the opponent's view of the serve. When the ball is served they move to their new positions. The switch should be made as soon as possible with both players alertly watching the flight of the ball. Occasionally the opponents will return the ball on the first or second contact, necessitating a quick adjustment to receive this return. If the opponents use a pass-set-spike pattern, the front-line players must be adequately positioned to perform their defensive assignments.

Strategy

Four-two offense: Strategy on good pass. Assuming the pass is easily reached by the setter and that both spikers are right-handed and of equal ability, the setter should more than fifty per cent of the time set to the on-hand (left-front) spiker. If, however, the off-hand (right-front) spiker is considerably stronger than the on-hand spiker, she should receive more than half of the sets. In neither situation, however, should all sets go exclusively to one spiker; this enables the opposition's center blocker to anticipate the direction of the set. At intermediate and advanced levels the setter should set in relation to the blocking capabilities and actions of the opponents. Refer to pages 35–36 in Chapter 3 for detailed considerations for the setter at the various levels of skill.

Poor pass. When the pass is poor and the setter has to struggle simply to reach the ball, she should make the easy set in the direction she is facing. The risk involved in being called for a "throw" or executing a poor set is not worth the potential advantage in setting to the on-hand or stronger spiker.

Four-two offense: Strategy when ball mispassed. Although ideally the front-row setter in a four-two system does all the setting, on occasion the serve is passed so far away from the front-row setter that she cannot get to the ball. In this situation the player nearest the ball should call "mine" and step in and set it. In the meantime the front-row setter should move off the net to a center front spiking position.

If the mispassed ball is nearest one of the two front-court spikers the spiker would ordinarily step in and set the ball cross court to her fellow spiker. However, in intermediate and advanced plays, if the setter (center front) had moved off the net and could spike well enough to be an offensive threat, then a set to her would be a second option. If the mispassed ball is between two front and back players, it is more desirable to have a backcourt player set a mispassed ball because the ball is frequently in front of her; therefore, as she moves for the ball her body weight is usually moving in the direction she wishes to set the ball. In addition, when a backcourt player sets, all front-court players are available as targets for the set.

Sets from the backcourt are difficult to spike. Therefore, when a mispassed ball is being set from a position near the center of the back-court, the majority of the time the set should go to the on-hand (left-front) spiker. If, however, the left-front spiker is very weak or the right-front spiker is left-handed, the ball could be set to the right-front position. When the mispassed ball is to the left or right side of the backcourt, the nearest player to the ball must set it cross court. A down-the-line set is too difficult for the spiker because she must watch the ball and then make a 180° turn as the ball passes over her head in order to be facing the opponent's court as she spikes.

In intermediate and advanced plays a backcourt set to the center front would be a possibility when (1) the center front is back off the net, ready to spike, (2) the set to the center front is an on-hand set, or (3) the player setting the ball is too weak to push the set cross court.

In situations in which the mispassed ball is between two backcourt players, the one facing the most advantageous direction for a front set should play the ball. An exception would be when one player is known to be a superior setter; perhaps she is the setter in the backcourt. Then she should call off the other player and set the ball.

A variation of the regular 4–2 offensive system is the International 4–2. The setter receives the pass in the right front position about eight feet in from the sideline. The advantage of this variation is that it provides the option of a middle or outside attack even through there are only two hitters. The disadvantages of the variation are the left front defense can cheat toward the middle and there is less margin for error on the pass than in the regular 4–2.

Figure 8.5. Five-one serve reception positions: setter right back.

The Five-One Offense

A five-one offense utilizes five spikers and one setter. When the setter is in the front row, the five-one offense is the same as a four-two offense. However, when the setter is in the back row, she runs into the front court on every play to set. This creates a multiple offense or offense in which all three front-row players are utilized as spikers. To make this system work, the setter must be fast, smart, set well, and have a great deal of endurance. The spikers should be able to hit well both on and off-hand, and *must* be able to pass the ball accurately. Accurate passes are essential because they enable the setter to set either regular or play sets to all three spikers. Accurate passing also enables the setter to get to the ball in as few steps as possible; therefore, fatigue is less likely to hamper her setting.

Serve Reception

Setter in the front row. When the setter is in one of the front-row positions, the formation or serve reception is the same as in the four-two offense.

Setter right back. When the setter is in right-back position on serve reception she assumes a position immediately behind and slightly to the right of the right front (figs. 8.5A and B). This position removes her from any responsibility for passing the serve since she is hidden behind the right front. She waits in this position until the ball is served, then runs to the right of the right front and toward the passing target to the right of the net's center. Her five teammates assume passing positions shown in Figures 8.5A and B and attempt to pass the ball to the passing area shown. Assuming the pass is a good one, the setter will have the option of setting on-hand or off-hand regular or play sets. Play

Figure 8.6. Five-one serve reception positions: setter center back.

sets are automatically called off if the pass is mishandled and the setter cannot reach the ball, otherwise the designated play is run. In either event, after the setter sets the ball she moves to cover her spiker, then returns to the backcourt to play defense. Her exact defensive position depends upon the type of defense employed and the relative defensive abilities of the other two backcourt players.

Setter center back. The serve reception positions for the five-one offense with the setter in the center-back position are shown in Figures 6.8A and B. This time the setter is behind and to the right of the center front. As soon as the ball is served she follows the path shown in the diagram to the passing target area and turns to face the left sideline and her two on-hand spikers. From this position she has the same setting options as when she was right back. If the server repeatedly serves into the switch, the setter may make her movement to the left of the center front.

Setter left back. When the setter is in the left-back position the team's serve reception formation is shown in Figures 6.9A and B. This is a difficult position for the setter. If the ball is passed off-center right the setter has to run two-thirds of the way across the court and turn around to face her two on-hand spikers. This is a long distance to cover in a short amount of time. Virtually all setters have difficulty with this movement, particularly if the serve is not accurately passed.

One solution is to pass to the left of center on serve reception only. Although this forces the setter to face two off-hand spikers, it does allow her ample time to reach the ball and make a good set.

A second solution is to use the four-player serve reception pattern shown in Figure 8.8. This formation places the setter closer to the net, allowing her

Figure 8.7. Five-one serve reception positions: setter in left back.

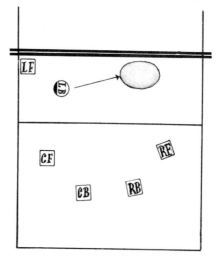

Figure 8.8. Five-one offense: alternate serve reception when setter is left back.

time to reach the right-of-center passing area and face her two on-hand spikers. It should be used only if the four remaining passers are strong serve receivers, since each has a greater area than normal to cover. The short center of the court is particularly vulnerable. After the serve has been contacted the left front must move away from the net into good spiking position, and the center front must move forward and to the right to the center spiking position.

Ball service at setter. Frequently the opposing server aims her serve just to the side and in front of the front-row player the setter is hiding behind. By doing so the server hopes to create a situation in which the backline setter moves forward and reaches the aim point of the serve at the same time as the ball, forcing her to pass the ball and forcing someone else to set.

This problem is best solved by having the setter stand directly behind her corresponding front-row player and randomly alternate her move forward to the left or right. Usually an opposing team has only one or two servers sufficiently accurate to force the setter to make this adjustment. Therefore, the setter must remember who they are and need vary her movement forward only when they are serving.

Setter passes the ball. As described above, the setter is sometimes forced to pass the ball on serve reception. During a rally after the serve the setter's defensive positioning may also require her to make the first contact on the ball. There are many ways to handle these situations depending on the versatility and maturity of the players.

One is to utilize an auxiliary setter. Since the passing pattern of off-center to the right is already set up, the setter would also pass to that spot. The player in the right-front position would then set the ball since she would be near and facing two on-hand hitters.

A second solution is to have a technique player take over the setting duties. For each position in rotation in which the setter is in the backcourt a technique player is designated. This player is usually the right back or center back, whichever is the best setter. Any time she sees the setter passing the ball and knows she can get to the pass, she calls "mine" and moves to the front court to set the ball. This preserves the three front line players' spiking potential.

Setter gets tired. To set every ball in a two or three game match requires a lot of running. If the setter is not in excellent condition, or if the passes are off-target and force the setter to take extra steps to the ball, the quality of the setting and thus the total offense diminishes. If the setter is out of condition she should be substituted out of the game while she is in the fornt row. If poor serve reception passing is the cause of the setter's fatigue, the coach would do well to switch to a four-two offense until the passing improves. This will not only give the one setter some rest, but it may also lessen the confusion created by bringing in the setter from the backcourt. Once the passing fails there is little opportunity for the setter to be deceptive. On a bad pass she usually has only one safe set remaining. Thus the purpose of a multiple offense is defeated.

A

B

C

Six-Zero Offense   A six-zero offense utilizes a multiple attack on every play by always bringing a backcourt setter in to set the ball. A true six-zero offense requires six players who are accomplished passers, spikers, and setters. The serve receive line up is always as shown in Figures 8.5A and B. Since all players can set and since a setter moving to a good pass in a multiple offense is facing two on-hand hitters when she comes from the right-back position, the right-back player always sets in a six-zero.

A true six-zero is rarely used because few teams have six players who can consistently set regular and play sets with the accuracy required in a multiple offense.

Six-Two Offense   A six-two offense also makes a multiple attack possible on every play by bringing in a setter from the backcourt. However, personnel requirements are not quite as stringent as in the six-zero offense. Although all players must be able to spike, only two must be good setters. The two setter-spikers are lined up opposite one another, as in a four-two offense, but all three front-line players come away from the net to receive the serve (figs. 8.10A, B, C). As the ball is served, the back-row setter-spiker moves to the net from one of the three backcourt positions. Here movements and problems are the same as when the setter comes in from the backcourt in a five-one offense. Once again, auxiliary setters or technique players may need to be designated.

Covering the Spiker   Regardless of the offensive system employed or the skill level of the players, many offensive plays will result in the spiker hitting the ball into the opponent's block. Frequently the blocked ball returns immediately to the spiker's side of the net. Since the spiker is descending from her jump she is unable to make any attempt to play the ball. Therefore, on all attacking plays it is necessary to place the spiker's teammates in positions behind and to the side of her to recover any blocked balls that return to the spiker's side of the net. This practice is referred to as "covering" the spiker.

Innumerable combinations of positions to cover the spiker are possible, depending on the offensive and defensive systems used and the location of the set and the setter. However, all attempt to place the three nearest players in a semicircle one large step away from the spiker, and still assign the remaining area to the two players furthest away from the play. All should be in a low ready position with knees flexed (fig. 8.11). The most common covering assignments are discussed below.

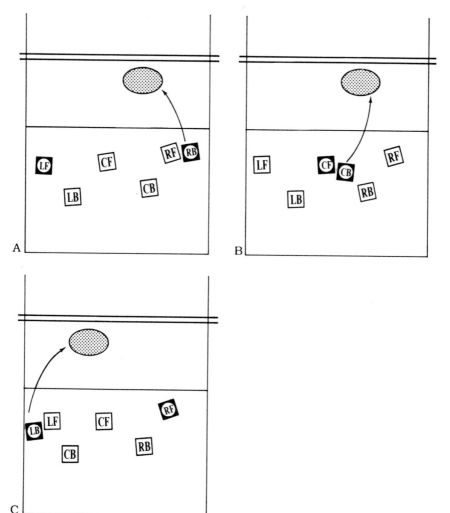

Figure 8.10. Serve reception positions for a six two offense.
A. Setter right back.
B. Setter center back.
C. Setter left back.

Four-two offense. When the left front is spiking, covering assignments are usually as shown in Figure 8.12. Note that the setter follows the direction of her set to cover the area to the right of the spiker. The left back moves forward to cover the area behind and to the left of the spiker. Regardless of how wide the set is she should not stand closer than two feet to the sideline. She can easily move from this position to the sideline in the time available. A move beyond the sideline is undesirable since a ball falling outside the court off the

Figure 8.11. Covering the right front spiker.

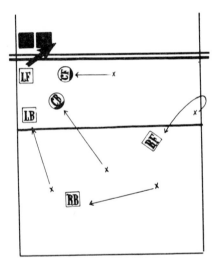

Figure 8.12. Covering the left front spiker: four-two offense.

block is a point for the spiking team. The center back moves forward to cover the area between the left back and the setter (center front). The right back moves to a deep position in line with the block, and the right front moves off the net to a position behind the ten foot line in the middle of the otherwise uncovered court area. When the set is to the right front covering assignments are reversed (fig. 8.11).

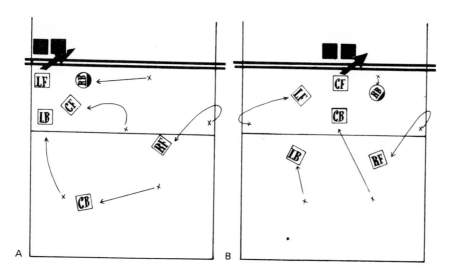

Figure 8.13. Covering spiker on multiple offense. A. Spiker in left front. B. Spiker in center front.

Multiple offense. Covering positions for multiple offenses are shown in Figures 8.13A and 8.13B. To avoid diagramming all possible combinations of coverage it was assumed that the setter played the right-back position on defense. It should be noted that the center set poses a particular problem in that the setter tends to be in line with and in front of the side spiker when covering. Any time a side spiker finds herself looking at the setter's back while covering, she should move further off the net since the setter is closer to the spiker and is accustomed to following her set to a covering position.

9

Defensive Systems

The basis of defense in volleyball, as in other sports, is to deploy the players into the areas of the court where the ball will come the highest percentage of the time. This should force opponents, as often as possible, to execute their least choice option in order to score. In order to select the appropriate defensive coverage it is important to know the opponents' capabilities to perform the techniques and tactics of the game.

Basic skill level will also be an indicator as to defensive positioning. No one basic defensive system can adequately cover all alternatives so that game situation adaptations may be necessary. For example, although the blocking defenses are considered basic for intermediate and advanced levels, there are times when an opponent will not be capable of aggressively spiking the ball. In these instances the blocking defense is called off in favor of either a "no block" or a "free ball" defense. It is conceivable that at beginning levels the opponents would never be a threat to spike aggressively, so that the "no block" defense (page 117) should be the basic defensive method employed.

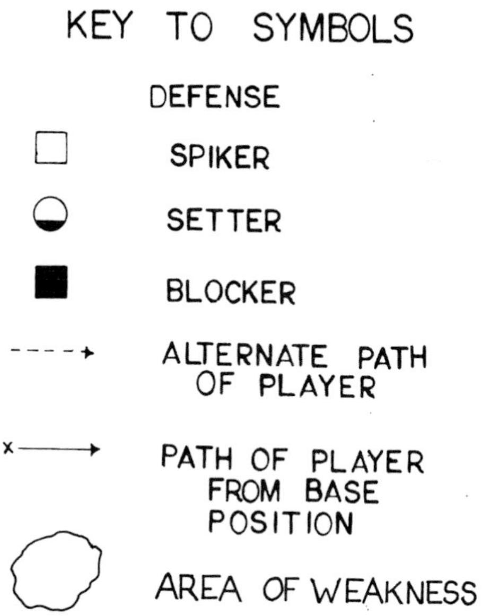

KEY TO SYMBOLS

DEFENSE

☐ SPIKER

◓ SETTER

■ BLOCKER

----→ ALTERNATE PATH OF PLAYER

x——→ PATH OF PLAYER FROM BASE POSITION

⬭ AREA OF WEAKNESS

Figure 9.1. Key to symbols.

Most teams use one of two basic defensive systems although variations of each are common, depending upon personnel of both offensive and defensive teams. The two most commonly used defenses are designated as the middle-back and the middle-up systems. Each defensive system is designed to cover a majority of the court space, forcing the offense to be deceptive or to execute their least choice option to be able to place the ball in a vulnerable court area.

Middle-up Defense

Strengths and Weaknesses

The strength of the middle-up defense lies in its good coverage of dinks and balls that come off the blocker's hands and fall behind the block. It also allows one weak backcourt defensive player to be hidden behind the block. Additionally, teams inexperienced in making the transition from defense to a multiple offense find it easiest to use a middle-up defense with the setter under the block.

The significant disadvantage of this system is that if the middle blocker is late or short, or if opponents are tall and can hit over the block, the deep center of the backcourt is wide open.

Front-Row Players

The base position for the front line on defense is with all three players in blocking ready position at the net (fig. 9.2). This position is taken by the serving team prior to service and as soon as the team's offense has returned the ball to the opponents in anticipation of defense.

When playing against a four-two offense or a multiple offense incapable of deception, the two-player block should always be used when the opponents have a potential of attacking the ball.

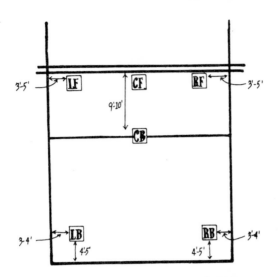

Figure 9.2. Base positions for middle-up defense.

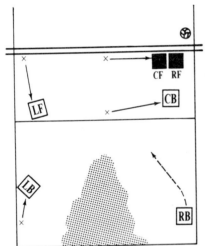

Figure 9.3. Middle-up defense against an on-hand spike.

Side double block. A side double block is formed by the front-line player opposite the spiker and by the center-front player (fig. 9.3A). The position of the side blocker depends primarily on the characteristics of the spiking styles of the opponents.

If the majority of the spikers or the two or three best spikers approach the ball in such good position that they can consistently spike the ball forcefully down the line, the block usually "takes the line." This means that the outside blocker positions herself so that her hands are in line with the ball's path down the line. In coaching terms, the outside blocker is "taking the whole ball." Figure 9.4A illustrates this concept.

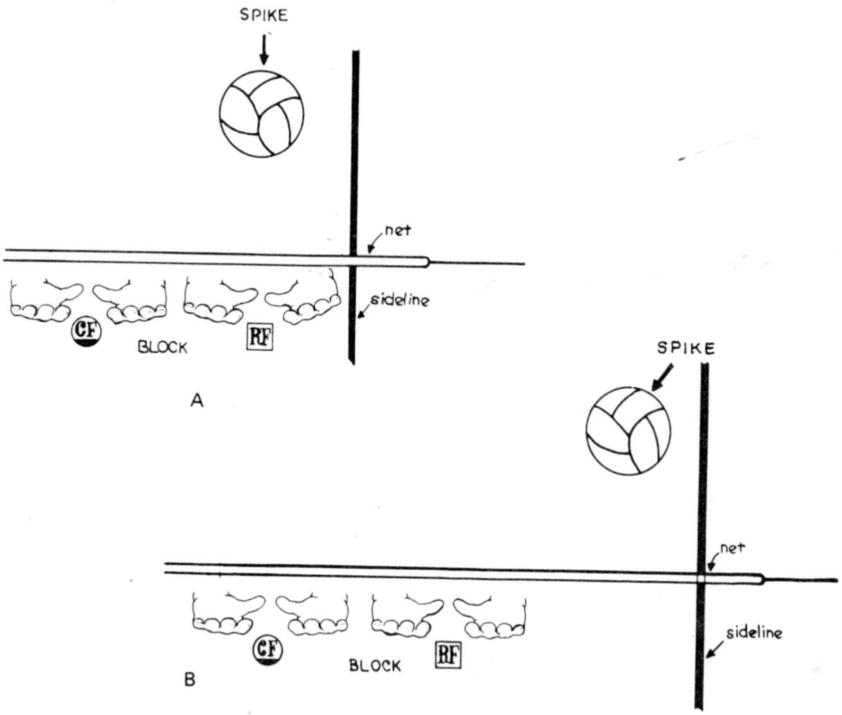

Figure 9.4. Double block. A. Taking the line. B. Giving the line.

The center front or middle blocker moves next to the side blocker and blocks out the immediately adjacent inside angle (fig. 9.4A). In order to attack the ball for a point the spiker is now forced to hit a cross-court angle, go over the block, use the block, or dink.

In situations where the attacking team is not able to spike the ball down the line consistently, the side blocker should "take the power angle" away from the spiker as the middle blocker blocks out the inside angle immediately next to the side blocker. This is illustrated in Figure 9.4B. Usually a little more line can be given off-hand than on-hand.

Center double block. A center double block is usually formed by the center front and the right front (fig. 9.5A). This combination blocks out the easy hit straight ahead and the powerful cutback to the defensive right side line. Some teams' center hitters, however, have difficulty controlling the cut back or are consistently so poorly positioned that they are unable to swing across their body. As a result they are better defended with a one-player block or by the left front, rather than the right front, joining the center front to take away the on-hand angle. One or more strong left-handed center spikers may also warrant a left front-center front block. In all center hit situations the blocker(s) must take away the straight ahead power spike so the center back can move to help her teammates defend the angles to the right and left of the block.

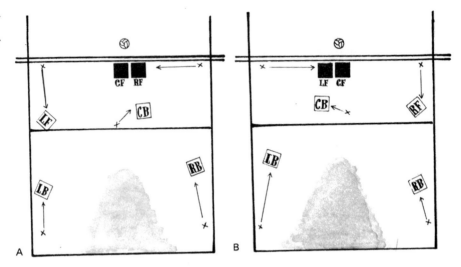

Figure 9.5. Middle-up defense against a center attack. A. Center front-right front block. B. Center front-left front block.

Nonblocking player. Whether against a side attack or a center attack, as soon as the nonblocking front-line player perceives that the direction of the set is away from her, she should back away from the net to the ten-foot line and one large step in from the sideline. As she moves backwards she should face the ball, watching the play form. Her exact position will depend on the relative position of the ball and the spiker to the net and the position of the blockers. She must be careful not to take balls high over her head since they will go out of bounds, nor should she reach for balls deep toward the back corner since these are better fielded by the backcourt player covering the crosscourt spiking angle.

Back-Row Players   The positions of the three back-row players are determined by whether the line is "given" or "taken." Basic to all positions are the concepts that (1) a player moves faster forward or laterally than backward and should, therefore, be positioned so that any ball not contacted by the block, approaching a player higher than her waist, is out of bounds, and (2) because of the position of the block there are areas of the court which are not accessible to the placement of a spike by the offense. The backcourt players are placed, then, in relation to the areas of the court which are open to opposing spikers for an unobstructed offense attacking play.

Base position. The base position for a middle-up defense is shown in Figure 9.2. Although these positions are simple, a common error of backcourt players is to creep in closer to the net than the positions shown. This practice often results in players having to move in the undesirable backward direction to play the ball because the play developed too fast for them to get back to their correct base positions.

As soon as the defensive players anticipate the direction of the set they should move to the base positions shown in Figures 9.3A and 9.5A or B.

Side attack coverage.

1. *Center back player.* From the center back base position on the ten-foot line the player moves laterally behind the block to a position between the two blockers. An exception to this occurs when the set is very near the sideline; in this situation the center back would never go closer to the sideline than the distance she can cover in one step (approximately four feet). From this position she is responsible for all dinks, as well as any balls deflected by the block which fall in front of the ten-foot line on her side of the court. However, half speed spikes or deflected blocked balls with any appreciable horizontal component of force passing higher than the center back's head should be allowed to go through to be played by the two backcourt players who are moving forward to play the ball.

When using this defense the blockers should be instructed not to reach back to play a dink or a ball off the block, as they will be taking the ball away from the center back who is in a much more balanced position to play the ball.

2. *Down-the-line player.* As shown in Figure 9.3, when the line is given the backcourt player on the line must hold in a deep position one step in from the sideline to guard against spikes down the line. However, if she sees that the spiker has committed herself to a cross-court hit she moves immediately toward the front and center of the court to help out with half-speed spikes and balls off the block that fall between the player in the under-the-block position and the deep cross-court player.

3. *Cross-court player.* The player responsible for defending against long angled on-hand cross-court spikes should be the best and fastest moving back-row passer of hard-hit balls since the greatest percentage of hard-spiked balls come into her area. She should assume a position off the inside shoulder of the middle blocker in line with the ball. Therefore, when both blockers and spiker are in the air she should be able to see both the spiker and the ball. Form this position she is responsible for balls both laterally and in front of her. If she finds the block obscuring her view of the spiker or the ball, then she has moved too far behind the middle blocker. She is also responsible for watching the middle blocker. If she sees that the middle blocker has been faked out of position or is late she gives up her position near the sideline and charges diagonally forward toward the center of the court.

However, in any situation in which the cross-court player is able to read the play and sees that the ball is headed deep toward the center, she is responsible for moving toward the middle to play the ball.

Center attack. If the opponents attempt to spike from the center position, the left back and the right back move forward so they can see the ball off the ouside shoulder of the blocker in front of them. If either sees that there is a hole in the block she would give up her deep position and move diagonally forward toward the center of the court to cover the higher percentage spike into the middle of the court.

The player-up moves off-center in the direction from which the side blocker came. For example, if the cutback is being taken away the right front is blocking so the player up moves slightly to the right. If the left front is blocking the player up would move to her left (fig. 9.5B).

Adaptations for off-hand spikers. The middle-up defense is essentially the same against on-hand and off-hand spikers. However, since spikers frequently trap themselves into hitting cross court on the off-hand side, the line defensive player may often find she is able to anticipate the cross-court hit and vacate her deep position for one closer to the net (fig. 9.3A reversed).

Middle-Back Defense

The advantage of the middle-back defense is that a player is placed in the backcourt to field spikes into the deep court area. This is especially useful when the opposing spikers are capable of consistently hitting the spikes past or over the block, or when the front-row players are inconsistent in forming an adequate block. The major weakness of this defense is its vulnerability to deceptive dinks, half-speed spikes, or any other spike falling off the hands of the blockers.

Strengths and Weaknesses

Front-Row Players

The positions and blocking responsibilities for front-row players for this defense are the same as described for the middle-up defense outlined on pages 109–114 above.

Back-Row Players

Base positions. The base positions for the middle-back defense are shown in Figure 9.6.

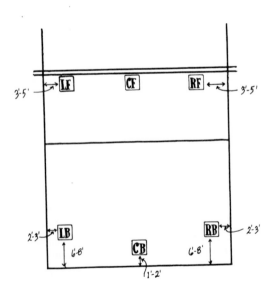

Figure 9.6. Base positions for middle-back defense.

Figure 9.7. Middle-back defense: double block against a side attack.

Side attack.

1. *Center back player.* The center back should be the team's strongest backcourt player. The center back base position (fig. 9.6) is in the center of the court, approximately one foot inside the end line. From here she moves laterally so that she is between the two blockers and in line with the ball. As long as the block goes up and is together, the center back's only move would be laterally for balls going over or deep off the hands of the blocker. An exception would be a half-speed hit or ball falling short off the block in the middle of the court. These are in the most vulnerable area of the center-back-deep defense, but a recovery must be attempted. Since the center back should be a very fast player and has a good view of the play forming, she should make an all-out effort to play the ball even if she thinks the left back or right back is slightly closer to the ball. Frequently a spectacular save or two on a difficult center ball is just the spark a team needs to encourage all team members to also make an all-out effort to play every ball.

When there is a hole in the block or the center blocker is late, the center back's prime duty switches from lateral movement to forward movement. In this situation she must charge forward to cover the hard spike in the middle of the court and hope that the less likely deep spike won't happen or can be reached by the left or right-back players.

2. *Down-the-line player.* If the block gives the line the backcourt line position is the same as in the middle-up defense. Frequently, since in the middle-back defense the deep center of the court is covered, the blocker takes the line, thus enabling the line player to move from her base position halfway up the line. By so doing she is able to move forward for dinks or laterally for balls off the block although if the side blocker fails to go up or the spiker hits over the block, the down-the-line corner is not covered. The risk can be minimized by having the tall player take the side blocking assignments, a situation that

Figure 9.8. Middle-back defense: double block against a center attack. A. Left front-center front block. B. Right front-center front block.

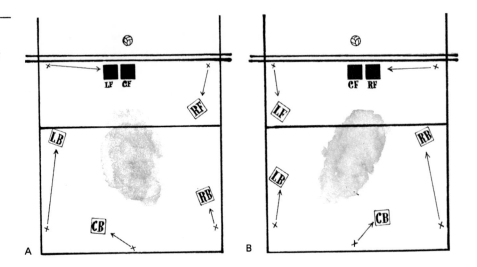

frequently happens anyway in a four-two offense. However, even with the center back player deep, a short middle blocker is a liability if the opponents utilize a multiple offense with a large percentage of center attack plays.

3. *Cross-court player.* The starting position is basically the same as in the middle-up defense, once again aligning herself off of the inside shoulder of the middle blocker. Since the center back player is deep the cross-court player no longer has to be concerned about balls going deep over or off the block and can, therefore, move one step closer to the net than in the middle-up defense. On a normal wide set the cross-court player is equidistant between the non-blocking front-row player and the center back. However, when a poor block forces the center back to charge forward the deep balls once again become the cross-court player's concern.

Center attack. The positions of the backcourt defensive players against a middle attack depends upon whether the right or left front is joining the center front to form the block. In either situation the backcourt player on the same side of the court as the side blocker moves into a position just off of that blocker's shoulder, three to four feet in from the side line (fig. 9.8A and B). The center back moves to a position directly behind the center of the block. It is her responsibility to move to any ball rebounding off of the block into the deep court area. If the block is not adequately formed she must charge forward to cover the vulnerable middle-court area. The backcourt player behind the non-blocking front-row player moves off the shoulder of the center blocker in order to field the ball hit past the block.

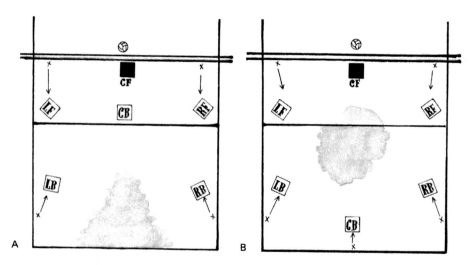

When the opponent's center attacks are so infrequent or so weak that they can be contained by one blocker, or when the opponents are so deceptive that the side blocker is unable to get to the center block, then the defensive alignment should be as shown in Figures 9.9A and B. Note that both the left and right fronts are off the net, just in front of the ten foot line and three to four feet from the sideline. The two deep backcourt corner defensive players are lined up along their respective sidelines off the shoulders of the center blocker.

In the middle-up defense the center back is on the ten foot line behind the center blocker. In the middle-back defense this player assumes a ready position at the center of the endline. If she sees that the middle blocker is not going up on the block she should rush forward toward the center of the court.

Single Player Block on Center Attack

When the opposing spiker receives a set to her left or right so far away from the net that she cannot aggressively attack the ball a block is of little value; the resulting spike will usually travel in an upward trajectory over or around the block, and descend with moderate velocity somewhere near or beyond the ten-foot line. As a result, this type of spike is best defended by moving the blockers away from the net into the "no block" positions shown in Figures 9.10 A, B through 9.11 A, B. As the blockers move away from the net they must remember to face the spiker and watch the ball. As the spiker contacts the ball players should have assumed the defensive ready position.

It should be noted that the "no block" positions in the four-two offense are the same in the middle-up and middle-back defenses. In the latter defense the center back can be aided in remembering to move forward by likening the situation to the one blocker or hole-in-the-block situations which also require her to move forward. When the middle-up defense is used in a "no block" situation with a multiple offense, the player behind the block must remember

No Block Situation

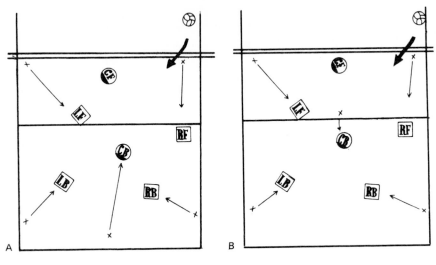

Figure 9.10. No block positions on four-two offense. A. Middle-back defense. B. Middle-up defense.

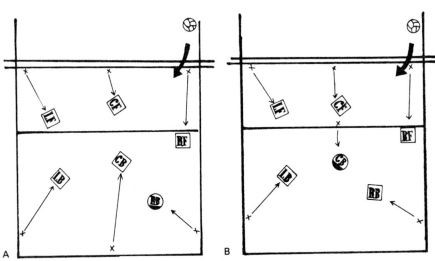

Figure 9.11. No block positions on multiple (five-one) offense. A. Middle-back defense. B. Middle-up defense.

to move back from her base position in front of the ten-foot line; otherwise she and the center front will be covering the same area, leaving the center of the court extremely vulnerable.

On a "no block" the setter in the multiple offense must remember that she first plays backcourt defense and then moves into the front court to set. Setters commonly, in error, prefer to think of the "no block" as a "free ball" play and run toward the front court as the blockers move back, leaving a large area of the court undefended. In the event the setter passes the ball, the auxiliary setter or backrow technique player must be alert to step in and set the ball. Refer to page 102 for a clarification of the auxiliary setter and technique player functions.

The "free ball" is a play in which the ball comes from the opponent's court in a recovery play. It is usually played over the net with the forearm or overhand pass from the middle or rearcourt, or from out of bounds. The flight of the ball is usually in a high trajectory into the middle of the court. The team receiving the "free ball" should anticipate it and call it whenever the opponents appear to be "in trouble" after the second contact, and assume a normal serve reception pattern.

The "free ball" is usually considered to be an offensive situation and is discussed as such for its offensive possibilities in the preceding chapter. Since in the "free ball" the arc of the ball is high, the objective is to set up a near perfect pass-set-spike attack. The first contact of the ball should be made with an overhand pass, whenever possible, because greater passing accuracy will usually result.

Ideally, defensive systems place players in the areas where opponents are most likely to hit the ball. However, to reach many balls the defensive player must still move rapidly since the area she covers is large relative to the amount of time the ball remains in the air. In many situations even the best thought out defensive systems are useless if the individual players are not able to anticipate the path of the ball's flight and move from their base positions toward it before the ball is contacted.

With experience players are able to anticipate the direction a ball will travel by watching the placement of the set relative to the net and the block, the timing, alignment, and approach angles of the spiker. Examples of the kinds of judgments players will learn to make are given below.

Distance of the set from the net. Assuming the spiker is in good alignment with the ball and has no block to contend with, a close set will most likely be angled sharply downward. The farther away from the net the set is, the deeper the spiker will be forced to hit the ball.

Angle of spiker's approach to the net. The less perpendicular the angle of the spiker's approach to the net, the more likely she will hit cross court. Although on a shallow approach in good alignment with the ball she may be able to cut the ball down the line on her on-hand side, she will not be able to hit down the line with power from her off-hand side.

Angle of spiker's shoulders and hips to net. Regardless of the angle of her approach, an on-hand spiker whose shoulders and hips are perpendicular to the net cannot hit the ball down the line. An off-hand player's chances of spiking down the line with any power are negligible from this position.

Alignment of spiker with ball. If the spiker has aligned so that the ball is nearer the sideline than her spiking shoulder she will be forced to turn the ball back towad the sideline. Conversely, if the ball is closer to the center of the net than the spiker's arm, either because she did not get to the ball or the set was pulled inside, she will hit cross court. If the spiker runs under the ball she will hit deep.

Timing. If the spiker is late getting to the ball she may dink.

Armswing. If an on-hand spiker in good alignment with the ball brings her spiking hand over her head on her backswing she probably intends to hit the ball cross court.

Block. If the block is up and obscuring your view of the ball it is unlikely that the ball will be spiked hard at you. It is also quite likely, unless you are at the center back in a middle-back defense, that you are out of position and should move to your left or right, depending upon which of the above factors you know exist.

10

Transitions and Interchanges

Many of the decisions made after techniques are taught and an offensive and defensive system selected are among the most important decisions made by the coach. Factors such as how the transition from offense to defense is made, and when and where players will interchange offensive and defensive positions, can make significant differences in a team's success. Important also are the decisions made by the coach during the game situations regarding line ups, substitutions, and timeouts. It is further essential that the performance of a team be evaluated to aid the coach in future decisions. This chapter attempts to identify some of these additional considerations in coaching a volleyball team.

Although offensive and defensive systems were explained in preceding chapters, no attempt was made to explain the movement of players from offensive to defensive positions. This explanation was intentionally avoided until now because it would be meaningless to a reader not familiar with both phases of

Transition From Offense to Defense

the game. The manner in which this transition is made depends on the offensive and defensive systems being combined, and the abilities of individual team members. The following discussion will be concerned only with transitions from systems of play; additional adaptations will be covered in the other sections.

Four-Two
Offense:
Transition to
Defense

Any transition from offense to defense should have an intermediary step in which the spiker is covered. Because the four-two offense is not a complex system the transition from offense to any defense, assuming all players are of equal ability, is simple. Following serve reception, the five nonspiking players move to cover the spiker. Assuming the spiked ball misses the block, all players then move to their base defensive positions. From the base positions they then adjust in relation to the formation of the opponent's offense. Either a block is formed or "no block" or "free ball" is called. On a "no block" or "free ball" the front-row players move off the net. Assuming a blocking situation exists, as soon as the blockers return to the court they must turn to follow the ball and assume their offensive roles; the spiker moves away from the net into her spiking ready position and the setter moves to set the pass.

Following her movement away from the net to play defense, the nonblocking spiker must also move to her spiking ready position. These movements complete the transition cycle.

The cycle is shortened on occasion when the ball is hit into the block and rebounds back into the spiker's court. Assuming that one of the covering players passes the ball, the offense must quickly regroup. Usually the covering player attempts to pass the ball to the centerfront position. Regardless of where the ball is passed the setter nearest the play sets one of the spikers who has once again moved away from the net and wide to be ready to attack. In the event the setter passes the ball from the covering position, a plan for the direction of her pass and an alternate setter to step in and set the ball must be established.

Multiple Offense:
Transition to
Defense

Due to the complexity of a multiple offensive system, transition problems are increased. Following serve reception and formation of an offensive play, the spiker is covered. The major coordination problem is to return the setter into the back row for defense. It is not necessary for the setter to return to her original position. She usually moves to the backcourt position from which she can most easily return to the setting position on a subsequent play. Assuming the spike does not contact the opponents' block, front-row players move to the base positions for the block. Back-row players also return to their defensive base positions. This procedure is relatively simple if a middle-up defense is used and the setter assumes the position behind-the-block. However, if the middle-back defense is in use, the setter must return to one of the deep backcourt positions following the cover. Therefore, it is highly desirable to switch the setter into the right-back position of defense, since this would place her on the right-hand side of the court from which she has the easiest return pathway to the setting position. When the setter is center-back, after the cover she moves into the right-back position for defense and the right back assumes the middle-back position. When the setter is left back, she covers the spiker from the setting position, moving from the cover to the right back as the other two back players move one position to their left.

The switching problems are greatly simplified when a team is serving. If the setter is not in the position which is most advantageous from which to make the defensive to offensive movement, she waits until the ball is served and then switches to that position. The other back-row players make the appropriate adjustments to accommodate this switch. In the middle-up defense the setter would move to center back; in the middle-back defense the setter would switch to the right back.

If, in the middle-up defense, it is found that the setter is forced to field numerous dinks on the first contact, consideration should be given to using another backcourt player in this position and switching the setter to the right back position.

Each player in the line-up must know her relative position to other players on the court and be certain to move back to original position prior to each serve.

Interchanging Positions

Offensive Interchanges

Interchanging offensive positions is often done to place offensive players in the position from which each can be most effective. The two most frequently used offensive interchanges or switches are explained below.

1. Switch the strongest front-row spiker into her preferred attacking position. Examples include: a right-handed player moving to the left front and a left-handed player moving to the right front to be on their on-hand spiking sides; a fast center spiker switching to center front so she can hit play sets out of the middle.
2. Switch a tall spiker in front of the short opposing blocker.

Offensive interchanges are easily accomplished when a team is serving. Players simply take positions near one another, being careful not to overlap positions or screen the opponents' view of the serve; when the ball is served, they move to their new positions.

When the team receiving serve desires to make an offensive change of positions, an offensive play and cover must first be completed before the switch can be made. If two players next to one another are to interchange positions and the ball is set to the side spiker involved in the switch, the procedure is simple; the ball is spiked and after the cover the two players exchange places as they move to their base blocking positions. If, however, the ball is set in the direction away from the side spiker involved in the switch, she will have to move a long distance to go from her covering position to her new position. This movement is not impossible, but both players involved must be alert to effect it as rapidly as possible.

When it is desirable for a player to switch from one side of the court to the other, involving a three player position exchange, most teams should attempt it only when their team is serving since the front line defense frequently deteriorates to the extent that the point is lost before any offensive play can be made.

Defensive Interchanges

Defensive interchanges of positions are made in both front and back line positions. Some of the front line defensive switches are as follows: (1) Switching a tall blocker in front of a tall, effective spiker; (2) Switching an experienced or fast blocker to the center-front position; (3) Switching an experienced side blocker opposite a deceptive side spiker.

Backcourt position interchanges are made for many reasons. One is to move the strongest backcourt defensive player into the most difficult backcourt position. In the middle-up defense, this would be the left back corner or cross-court angle from the opponent's on-hand spike. In the middle-back defense, this would be the center back position.

Backcourt interchanges are also made to move the weakest defensive player in the least demanding defensive position. In the middle-up defense, the next least demanding available position is the center back, or right back if the setter plays center back.

In the middle-back defense the weakest player would be switched to the right-back position. If, however, a multiple offense is employed and it is desirable to place the sitter in the right-back, the switching of the setter takes precedent. The second choice place to switch the weak player is to the left back.

Front line defensive position interchanges are accomplished in the same manner as offensive switches. Often defensive and offensive switches conflict, and the switch to the greatest advantage of the team must take precedence.

Backcourt defensive interchanges are easily effected when the team is serving. The two or three players involved move close together without overlapping positions, and as the ball is served they move to their desired position.

Defensive backcourt switching is more complicated when the team is receiving serve, in that the switching players must hold their positions until the ball is passed, cover the spiker, and then as they pull away from their covering positions, exchange defensive positions. Occasionally, if both players involved in a backcourt defensive switch are alert, switches can be made at the time the ball is passed before moving to cover positions. For example, if a team is using a four-two offense and a middle-back defense, when the best defensive player is left back it is desirable to switch her to center back. This would usually be accomplished by switching after the cover. However, if the center back passes the ball the left back may move behind her to back her up, and after the ball is passed call "switch," sending the passer to the left back.

It should be noted that although interchanging of positions is designed to strengthen a team's play, if players lack the experience to make these switches smoothly, the result will be confusion which will weaken rather than strengthen team performance. Although switching when a team is serving is not complicated, switching on serve reception should probably be reserved for advanced levels of play. Under no circumstances should a coach expect players to attempt offensive or defensive switches in a competitive situation if the players involved have not had extensive practice time to learn them, substitutes and starting line-up players alike.

Part Four

Coaching Considerations

11

Coaching Administration

The coach of a volleyball program will spend a good deal of time and energy as an organizer and administrator. The focus of the following sections is on coaching in schools and colleges because these situations often demand extensive coordination with other areas of the institution. Much of the content, however, may have application for coaching club, recreation, and service teams.

A Coaching Philosophy — The success of the volleyball program is measured in relation to the intent when the program was begun. What are the purposes of women's competitive volleyball? How can these purposes be best realized? These questions should be continually asked as the coach proceeds in her task.

To most players the bases for success are the personal satisfactions that are gained during performance on the court and associations made off the court. The personal satisfaction comes from knowing one has played well, from the interrelationships with people, and from being a part of a well-coordinated team effort.

The coach must approach the volleyball program with goals to be accomplished and with a philosophy of coaching which will give direction to the way in which these goals are approached.

The following are suggested for consideration:

1. The volleyball programs in schools and colleges are for the students of the institution. Players' responsibilities and functions as students are primary.
2. The volleyball program is for the participant. Her needs, interests, and desires should be the basis of all decision-making. Her health and welfare are to be given primary consideration. Her role as a woman in society must be respected and maintained.
3. The volleyball program offers the participant a broad educational experience—a total experience. It is, or can be, much more than the acquisition of skill or the participation in volleyball matches. The extent to which it is more depends on the leaders of the program.
4. Each participant, if she so desires, should be challenged to reach her potential as a player.
5. Each participant should be respected as a worthy person. Skill level should not determine the interest or attention given a player.
6. All volleyball teams should be coached by competent coaches who keep abreast of trends and techniques of the game.

The authors have used the premises above as the basis for conducting a volleyball program. These statements are offered not as absolutes, but as an illustration of the type of thought and consideration which the coach should make prior to initiating a program. Establishment of basic beliefs about the program will aid in decision-making in all phases of action and will lend consistency to it.

Personnel— Coordination and Management

Coaching Staff

Most volleyball programs are under the direction of a single coach. However, consideration may be given to expanding to a staff of coaches. The number of coaches will depend on the number of players and their skill levels, and the anticipated function of each coach.

If two or more coaches form a staff, a delineation of duties and responsibilities must be made. Duties can be divided according to techniques, offense and defense, or each coach can be assigned to work with specific teams. During practices each coach should be actively involved in the coaching function and share responsibilities of working with the players. A coach should be more that a statistician, an equipment supervisor, or an observer.

Since the advent of scholarships at the college level, scouting and recruiting are coaching responsibilities that demand considerable time and energy. It is helpful if the coaching staff can share these responsibilities.

To coordinate the staff, frequent meetings are necessary. If each coach is responsible for a team it is often helpful to review the practice and game plans with other coaches to gain ideas and verify thinking. If a team coaching approach is used and the same player will be instructed by various coaches at different times, it is important that the staff totally agree as to the execution of techniques and strategy. One coach should never contradict another in the presence of a player.

Selection of Team Members

Before the season starts the coach must make a number of basic decisions. Some questions to be considered are:

1. Shall there be a restriction on the number of participants? Why? How?
2. For whom is the program? All interested? Highly skilled?
3. How many teams will be formed? Size of teams? Why?
4. If there is more than one team, will teams be classified as to level (V, JV)? If so, to what degree will mobility from team to team be possible (league rules, etc.)?
5. Will newcomers have equal opportunity to be considered for teams with returning players? How will this be assured?
6. What procedure will be used to screen and classify players? Will potential for improvement be considered?
7. How much orientation to skills and systems of play will occur before selection?
8. Will players participate in establishing the screening process? In evaluating performance? Which students? To what degree?

A careful study of these and similar questions will help to establish a format for screening and selection. It may be helpful to enlist participant reactions to these questions before the screening takes place.

A plan for publicizing the beginning of the volleyball program is essential. The publicity should include time and place of the screening and a brief overview of the extent of the program. A published schedule of practice times and matches will motivate interest in the program, not only for those who wish to participate, but for those who may wish to assist as volunteer help or attend the matches. Also, this form of communication will lessen the likelihood of players trying out who are not free to meet the schedule.

Participants should be thoroughly informed of all the factors in the screening process, such as number of teams, size of teams, anticipated personnel make-up of each team (spikers and setters), and procedure for announcing the results.

An interdependence exists between the decisions in screening and grouping of players into teams and the selection of offensive and defensive systems. Ideally, team members would be selected and offense and defense systems employed to suit the capabilities of the players. However, after the potential starters are selected some additional considerations are necessary to select the substitutes.

First, mobility of the strongest spikers to block and play back court defense must be studied. If the spikers are strong all-around players, substitutes who have like abilities might be chosen. If any potential starting spiker is weak defensively, it might be wise to select a back-up spiker who is a strong defensive player. It is also possible to select a substitute who will serve as a defensive specialist.

Setters have often developed their ability to handle the ball well because they have either lacked the height or jumping ability to spike, or have played coeducational volleyball and have not had opportunity to block or spike. Whatever the reason, the short setter may be a liability as a front-line blocker. Therefore, the coach must weigh the asset of her "good hands" against the liability of her potentially weak blocking. The coach should also consider her potential for improving her jump. She may be able to compensate for her lack of height by increasing her ability to jump.

Consideration for the selection and use of specialists must be made with care. Examples of specialists include a fast defensive player used only in the back row, a tall blocker used only against the opponent's strongest spiker, or a strong server who stays in the game only as long as she keeps her serve. The player who is selected to this role must understand it and accept it. Morale problems may arise if the specialist plays infrequently or if the team fails to appreciate the importance of her role. The selection of a specialist to a team is a doubtful practice if the starting team members have all-around playing abilities.

The announcement of team selections should be done promptly according to preannounced plans. Teams should be posted in alphabetical order. Players often have an inclination as to their status and placement, but few wish to have the teams announced before the group. The coach should let it be known that she is available to discuss selection decisions with all players.

The organization of a team begins with the selection of the team. Before the team was selected each candidate should have been aware of the general expectations for the group for the season. However, when the team is finally selected a number of specific expectations need to be established. These become the standards and policies for the functioning of the team. Player participation in establishing policies and standards is most desirable. If a person has participated in establishing a policy and consents to it, she will be much more inclined to be self-directed toward maintaining it.

Organizing the Team—Establishing Expectations and Standards

As soon as possible after the selection of the team a meeting of the group should be held. This time the coach presents an outline of objectives and policies regarding (1) practices, (2) matches, (3) conditioning and health practices, (4) attendance, (5) dress and clothing, (6) conduct, and any other subjects pertinent to the situation. A review of each should be made with an opportunity presented to modify the policy, if it is possible. Due to league and institutional rules, some policies regarding eligibility, insurance, travel, are not negotiable. At times, a coach's previous experiences or knowledge of situations beyond that of the players may necessitate her making decisions without consulting the teams. This should be done only in extreme instances, and at all times the teams should be given the supporting reason for the decision.

Since volleyball is a team game, the joining into the game means the joining of a team. This places the player in a position of giving up some individuality. When a player joins a team she should be aware that her individuality will be somewhat restricted by the common best interests of the group. If policies established have the endorsement of the majority of the team, a player, as a member of that team, should be expected to adhere to these policies without modification. It is the responsibility of the coach to preserve each player's individuality to the greatest degree possible through her methods of coaching and dealing with players. It is the responsibility of each player to accept the policies of her team and to follow them without asking for special consideration.

Establishing Channels of Communication

The team which has established its objectives by mutual agreement between players and coach is prepared to function as a unit. It is usually the role of the coach to set up the methods by which a team will attempt to meet its goals. However, it is helpful to consult with team leaders from time to time to evaluate the methods being used. This communication assists the coach in assessing the effectiveness of the methods being used and may give indication of a need to further explain or modify practice procedures, use of personnel or other factors. The sensitive coach will often be aware of the need for change and can use the evaluation sessions to test her own thoughts and establish alternatives for change in procedures.

Individual player problems or problems of player interaction can occur on any team. It is most desirable for players to feel free to approach the coach directly to ask questions or to ask for assistance in dealing with these problems. The fair and honest coach will be objective and impartial in dealing with problems, yet should be understanding and sympathetic. Often the shy or hypersensitive player will hesitate to come directly to the coach with her concerns. It should always be possible for players to bring their problems to team leaders who may work out solutions independently or bring the concerns to the coach. Both of these channels of communication should be well-known to all the players and every attempt should be made to keep them functioning.

Developing Responsible Team Membership

Team members should be prepared to share areas of responsibility within the volleyball program. Areas of individual responsibility include: attendance and punctuality at practices, meetings, and matches; meeting scheduled deadlines; attending to posted announcements or instructions; care and prompt return of issued equipment and clothing; and knowing and following all policies. Areas of group responsibility include: assisting with the setting up of facilities and controlling equipment during practices and matches; greeting opposing team members and officials at matches; providing moral support for team members and other teams in the program during practice and competition; assisting as scorers, timers, and linesmen for matches of other teams within the program.

A positive and enthusiastic approach toward these factors and early orientation of team members to the expectations for each individual as a part of the group will assist not only in the smooth functioning of the program, but will provide students with an enriched experience.

The most significant role of leadership on a team is that of the team captain. This duty may be shared by co-captains. Procedures for selecting the team captain vary. The team may elect the captain or the coach may appoint the captain. The choice of procedure depends somewhat on the background and experience of the team members and the proposed function of the team captain. The practice of appointing game captains and rotating the responsibility from player to player is also used. If the team captain is to have an ongoing function during the season, this latter practice has little value.

Developing Team Leadership

Among the duties which a captain might assume are:

1. Consultation with the coach regarding procedures for the season.
2. Consultation with coach regarding line-ups and use of substitutes.
3. Providing leadership for team organization at practices and during games.
4. Representation of the team whenever this is necessary. This includes greeting and thanking officials and opposing teams.
5. Providing moral support and encouragement for all teammates and encouraging team unity.
6. Being available to any teammate as a line of communication to the coach.

A well-organized program will provide an opportunity for team members to function as leaders. Whether all leadership roles are filled by players or not must be given consideration. If the schedule of practices and matches is extensive it may be undesirable for time-consuming duties to be made the responsibility of a player. If the schedule is limited, it may be possible and highly desirable for all duties to be assumed by team members. Leadership roles in the volleyball program might include: business coordinator; equipment coordinator; game preparation coordinator; travel arrangements coordinator; hospitality and social functions coordinator; publicity coordinator; or any other which might assist in making the team experience an enriching one.

To insure that the objectives of the program are met, careful planning of the total season and anticipated experiences should occur.

Planning for Practice and Play

The match schedule should be set well in advance of the start of the season. It is motivating to students to know that a schedule is planned, providing a real objective for the preparation and conditioning phase of the season. Also,

Match Schedule

students should know the days of the week and hours necessary for matches so that their plans for classes and student life can be coordinated to the best advantage.

The number of matches and length of season are determined by a number of factors, including the philosophy of the program, the budget available, and the availability of opposing schools to be scheduled.

Matches should be scheduled with a minimal amount of interference with students' class schedules. The spacing of matches is important. Occasionally it may be necessary to schedule back-to-back matches without practice time in between. This eliminates the possibility of making adjustments in practice, and as a scheduling technique should be evaluated in relation to the students' ability to deal with it.

Early season scheduling of scrimmage matches has proven to be an effective procedure. The scheduling of seven to ten games with an opponent of like ability, using a squad comprised of the potential first and second teams, allows both teams to use a variety of combinations of players. By mutual agreement, each team starts its weakest line-up and progresses to its strongest line-up throughout the course of the match. These games need not be officiated. This scrimmage match allows the coach to see all the players in a competitive situation before final team selections are made.

The first match of the season should occur only after students have had an opportunity to gain a degree of conditioning and learn the basis of their team systems. This usually can be accomplished in about twelve to eighteen hours of practice time.

Tournaments which are scheduled over a one- or two-day period are a good experience for a team. However, care should be taken in scheduling to avoid crowding such a tournament too closely to other matches. The concentration of play time will require the student to give up some study time and may also cause a degree of fatigue. Both factors make it advisable to allow a little time following the tournament before scheduling another match.

Master Schedule A total calendar should be developed which includes all practices, matches, and other pertinent dates. The calendar should be filled in with projected dates and times for:

1. screening period
2. physical examination
3. conditioning progression
4. deadlines for phases of developing offense and defense
5. paper work deadlines
6. picture taking
7. meetings
8. issuing and return of equipment and uniforms
9. travel departure and return

A breakdown of the season into practices, times, and their relationship to specific matches should be made. An outline of the specific content of each practice is important in order to accomplish specific goals at the projected time. This plan would include the allocation of time and area of emphasis for conditioning, skill development, offensive and defensive team work for each practice session.

Master Practice Plan

Each practice session should be carefully planned with regard to specific areas of concentration. The plan should include time allotments, assignment and grouping of players, specific procedures, and rotations. It is important that practices vary with their specific purposes. Preseason practices should emphasize conditioning and skill development, with progressions to develop the basic offenses and defenses to be used during the season. Practices during the season should include reinforcement of sound skill performance and conditioning, practice on individual player skill needs within the offense and defense used, refinement of team offense and defense, correction of weakness demonstrated in recent matches, work on game situation problems according to needs demonstrated in matches, and establishment of the game plan for the next match.

Practice Plan

Effective use of time during practices is essential. This can be accomplished through planning and experience in the use of given methods. The approach which has proven successful is that of dividing the practice into routines and progressions. Routines would be those things which must be accomplished at each practice in order that certain objectives are met, such as warm-up, conditioning, announcements, and basic skill rehearsal. Progressions would give practice in those factors which are built throughout the season, such as the adaptation of skills necessary to meet game situation demands, and the ability of the team to function under varying circumstances.

The length of time spent on any phase of practice depends on the intensity of the work effort required and the ability of players to maintain concentration and interest in the activity. Practice procedures which vary in intensity and difficulty should be used. Short periods of meaningful work seem to be most advantageous in preventing boredom and maintaining a high level of interest.

All players should have equal opportunity to participate in each phase of practice. When working on team patterns it is often easier to concentrate the practice with the starting line-up, while allowing substitutes to watch or simulate opponents. However, if substitutes are to be expected to feel like team members and to be able to perform with confidence and effectiveness when called upon, it is important that they be incorporated into each phase of practice in a meaningful way.

A minimum amount of player's time should be spent waiting for a turn to participate in any phase of practice. Three factors govern the choice of procedure in this matter. The first is that of player interest and concentration. The second is that of the intensity of effort required, and the third is the amount of individual coaching needed to perform well. To avoid boredom caused by waiting, it is suggested that a number of practice stations be used with a minimum number of players assigned to each station. When the intensity of the work effort is high, fewer groups with a larger number of players per group will allow a reasonable recovery time for those who have completed the work before having another trial; therefore, the waiting time is more meaningful and justified. If coaching is required for sound performance, players waiting may be listening and learning from watching the teammate practice. A judgment about the relative effects of each of these factors should be made before deciding upon the specific grouping and time allotments.

Checklists for Planning and Work Detail Much detail in planning has been recommended for conducting a program of competitive volleyball. In order that the planning becomes a reality, a number of administrative procedures are necessary. These are presented in the appropriate checklists given below.

Checklist: **Match Scheduling**

_____   Receive Budget allocation

_____   Identify anticipated costs of essential expenditures—allocate budget

_____   Clear facilities

_____   Plan calendar of holidays, vacations, major campus events, final examinations, etc.

_____   Schedule league matches

_____   Schedule practice matches, and tournaments

_____   Write letters of confirmation for all matches

_____   Receive written confirmation for all matches—(contracts)

_____   Publish schedule to school

_____   Release schedule to local news media

_____   Schedule officials

_____   Confirm facilities for schedule

Checklist: **Before Season**

_____   Confirm schedule

_____   Confirm facilities for schedule

_____   Order equipment

_____   Plan Master Schedule

_____   Confirm officials

_____   Set up physical examinations

_____   Publicize screening and try-outs

_____   Recruitment of players

_____   Awarding of scholarships

_____   Secure meeting rooms for team meetings

_____   Set up procedure for issuing uniforms

_____   Arrange for team pictures, individual pictures

Checklist: **Before a Home Match**

_____ Confirm officials
_____ Order payment for officials
_____ Order facilities to be cleaned—before/after
_____ Order bleachers to be set up
_____ Order visitor parking permits
_____ Send visitor parking permits
_____ Arrange for news releases
_____ Arrange for scorers, timers, linesmen
_____ Arrange for crowd supervision
_____ Arrange for visiting team
       _____ Locker room
       _____ Security of valuables
       _____ Towels
       _____ Privacy
       _____ Greeting
       _____ Hospitality
_____ Arrange for officials
       _____ Greeting and hospitality
       _____ Locker room
       _____ Security of valuables
       _____ Payment
_____ Arrange for team schedule
       _____ Issue uniforms
       _____ Arrival time in locker room
       _____ Arrangements for training and taping procedure/schedule
       _____ Set time to begin warm-up
       _____ Announce warm-up routine
       _____ Arrange for team meeting before/after match

Checklist: **Before an Away Match**

_____ Order equipment for travel
_____ Order training supplies for travel
_____ Order funds for travel: mileage, food, lodging, officials
_____ Arrange for transportation
_____ Arrange for lodging
_____ Plan itinerary
_____ Arrange for laundry of uniforms—if necessary
_____ Arrange team schedule
       _____ Issue uniforms
       _____ Issue itinerary with information about lodging
       _____ Announce arrival time for departure
       _____ Announce return time

_____ Review policies of conduct during travel
_____ Announce procedures for dealing with expenses
_____ Announce specific travel procedures

Checklist: **Facilities**

_____ Inspect floor surface
_____ Inspect standard mountings for safety
_____ Inspect seating arrangements
_____ Order schedule for cleaning before and after matches
_____ Order seating arrangement before and after matches
_____ Order placement of scorers' table and officials' stands for matches
_____ Order placement of score boards

Checklist: **Equipment and Supplies**

_____ Order practice and game balls
_____ Check nets; order replacements if necessary
_____ Check standards; order repairs if necessary
_____ Arrange for set up of nets for practices, matches
_____ Establish routines for and order periodic cleaning of balls and check inflation of balls
_____ Establish a standing order for practices
_____ Establish a standing order for matches
_____ Order training supplies
_____ Establish standing order for training kit for each practice
_____ Establish standing order for periodic replenishing of training kit

Checklist: **Player Information**

_____ Name, address, phone (both local and permanent)
_____ Parent or guardian
_____ Class schedule
_____ Prior experience
_____ Honors
_____ Health clearance, record
_____ Uniform sizes, game uniform and warm-ups, kneepads

Checklist: **Yearly Team Information File**

_____ Schedule
_____ Match results—master listing and score books
_____ Statistics
_____ Picture
_____ Copy of all news reports
_____ Roster and pertinent information regarding players' performance during season

12

Coaching Strategy

A good coach possesses the ability to make objective decisions prior to the match as well as during the competition. All coaching instruction should be expressed in an organized, confident and positive manner. The attitude of the coach will likely be reflected in the attitudes and performance of the players.

Of primary concern in coaching strategy are decisions related to game situations such as line-ups, time-outs and substitutions. Directly related to these concerns is the evaluation of performance.

Game Situations

Line-Ups

The coach must consider many factors when deciding on a line-up. It should be recognized that no single line-up will be able to incorporate all the alternatives suggested in the starting line-up positions prior to using it in a competitive situation. Many coordination errors can be avoided if players are accustomed to their positions and are moving in relation to the same players next to them. The following are suggested as guidelines for the determination of a line-up:

Four-two Offense

1. One setter must be in the backcourt and one in the front with two spikers between them. This insures the presence of one front-line setter in every rotation.
2. If two spikers are stronger than the other two, they are usually placed opposite each other in the line-up. This insures one strong spiker in the front court at all times.
3. If the one or two strong spikers can spike best from the on-hand side, they should lead the setter next to them in the line-up. This results in switches which will allow them to spike twice from the on-hand side and once from the off-hand side.
4. If a spiker is left handed, she should follow the setter next to her in the line-up. This will enable her to spike twice from her on-hand side.
5. If a spiker prefers the setting of one setter to the other, that setter should be the one closest to her in the line-up. This usually happens when one setter sets higher or lower than the other. Tall spikers or slow spikers usually prefer higher sets than spikers with fast approaches.
6. A player with an extremely strong serve should be first or second in the line-up so that she rotates into the service position as often as possible in a game.
7. If a team starts the game receiving serve and the rules do not require a rotation before the first serve, the strongest spiker should be in the left front, and the front-row setter should be right front. This places the strong spiker on her on-hand spiking side for all play during the first five side-outs, and in the front row for the first seven side-outs.
8. If a team starts the game receiving serve and must rotate one position before its first serve, the strongest spiker should begin in the left-back position, with the front row setter in the center front. This enables the stronger spiker to hit twice from her on-hand side, and remain in the front row during the first six side-outs after her team first serves.
9. If a team serves first, the strongest spiker usually starts in the left-front position and the front row setter in the right-front position.
10. If opponents have one extremely strong spiker, place the best blocker in the line-up so that she is in the front row at the same time as this spiker for as long as possible.

Multiple Offense. In addition to the basic considerations above regarding strong spikers, servers, and blockers, the following should be remembered when using a multiple offense.

1. When using a five-one offense, the setter usually starts in the right back when her team serves first. This results in the greatest number of multiple offense plays before the setter gets to the front row and the offense becomes a two-spiker system.

2. When using a six-two offense, the back-row setter usually starts in the right back since this is the easiest position from which to move into the setting position.

The coach must be prepared to use substitutions wisely in order to serve the team's purposes to greatest advantage. Prior to the season decision must be made as to the basic use of substitutes.

Substitutions During a Match

Purposes. A number of reasons exist for using substitutes during a match. These include: (1) to eliminate a weakness; (2) to capitalize on special abilities; (3) to rest a starting player; (4) to replace an injured player; (5) to allow substitutes to gain experience; and (6) to gain a psychological lift or advantage.

Additional Factors. There are many implications for team unity and morale related to the substitution procedure. These should be considered carefully alongside the strategic use of substitutes.

Substitutions should be made to eliminate weakness on the court. If a starting player is playing below her potential and hurting the team effort, she should be substituted for a stronger player on the bench, if one is available. However, the coach should not remove a player of proven ability from the game when she makes her first mistake. The coach must show faith in the player by leaving her in until she has had a reasonable chance to prove herself. Otherwise, players play so cautiously for fear of making one error and being removed from the game that they play consistently below their practice level of performance.

Substitutes should practice in the same positions they will be expected to play when used in the game. If a substitute spiker will be used in place of a spiker who hits twice from the middle and once offhand, and who plays defense once in center back and twice in left back, she should practice this position with the other starters to familiarize herself with the movements and their coordination with the other players. Most importantly, she should be familiar with this position when she goes into the game. It would be foolish to substitute this player for a setter, just as it would be to substitute a setter in the front court for the number one spiker.

It is natural for substitutes to want to get into the game. However, they should be a positive influence while on the bench. Rather than complaining to each other about not being in the game because player X on the court is playing poorly, they should be rooting for their teammates on the court. A coach can do much to eliminate such complaints by letting substitutes know when they can expect to be used and then doing so.

Although it is desirable for morale reasons to use all of the substitutes during the course of the game this may not always be possible. When behind, the practice of putting a substitute into the game just so she can have a chance to play is questionable if any hope of winning remains. When winning easily, substitutes can be used. However, if this is the only time a player ever goes into a match the player may become disheartened. Each substitute should have experience playing when the result of the game is in the balance.

No more than two, or at the most three, substitutes should be placed on the court at the same time unless the opponents are extremely weak. If all six players on the court are substitutes and the team begins to lose, loss of confidence is quite possible. If players are put into the game one or two at a time, the first team players remaining maintain sufficient continuity to control play and allow the substitutes to play their best and gain confidence.

Instructing Substitutes. The player going into the game should have been properly instructed. She should know who she is going in for and how to legally make the substitution. If there are instructions to be given to team members she should know them clearly and convey them as soon as she enters the court. It is best to keep instructions simple for the inexperienced player. Too much detail will confuse her. Direct, positive statements made in a manner which shows confidence in the player will aid her in feeling sure of herself as she enters the game.

Team Adjustment to Substitutes. When a substitute enters the game, players on the court should be ready to listen in case she has information to share. They should also be prompt to verbally greet her and assist by reminding her of coverage, interchanges, or other coordination factors which require orientation. The setter should remember to allow a substitute spiker some "warm-up" to the game before setting to her.

Time-Outs When a volleyball team is consistently gaining points over the other team and not behind, time-outs are rarely taken. Even if players on the winning team are tired, they are usually better rested through substitution than a time-out, since time-outs are extremely short, ranging from 30 seconds to one minute. The brief lapse of time might also break the winning momentum or allow the opponents to regroup to improve play.

When a team is behind or losing ground, wise use of time-outs can reverse the trend of the match. Since only two time-outs may be taken during the game, the coach must take note of how many she has used. Time-outs should be considered in the following situations:

First Time-Out.

1. Use a time-out to attempt to stop an opposing server from making a run of points as a result of poor passing. During this time-out, adjustments in the formation for serve reception should be made.
2. Use a time-out to stop play at scores such as 7–0, 8–1, 9–2. Even if the team is not consistently making the same errors, sometimes a break at this point relaxes tensions. A word from the coach saying "keep it simple

and play your own game" may be all the team needs. If, on the other hand, the team is behind because of lazy play, this may be the time to suggest that whatever happens on the court, "a ball should not touch the floor before a player does."

Second Time-Out. The second time-out is rarely used before the opponents have scored eight or nine points, and is usually saved until the opponents have scored eleven or twelve points. Prior to this stage there is always the hope that the tide of the game will turn without calling a time-out. The second time-out, late in the game when the team is well behind, should be called while there is some chance of recovery, no later than the opponent's twelfth or thirteenth point.

When a team is ahead but the score is almost certain to be tied at twelve, thirteen, or fourteen all, the second time-out may be used to attempt to prevent the score from being tied.

The reader is referred to page 142 for brief discussion regarding the use of time-outs to coach for improving individual player performance.

Throughout the season the coach is involved in various forms of judging, measuring, and recording the performances of individual players and the team. This is done in order to identify areas of need for growth and practice. It is also done to better insure that valid decisions are made regarding the appropriate use of personnel and the effectiveness of team functioning within the offensive and defensive systems used.

**Evaluating
Performance**

Purposes

Individual Player Information. The coach should have an accurate assessment of the ability of each player to perform the techniques and strategies of the game. Progress of the player is important to chart since it may be a factor in determining her potential for increased value to the team. Lack of progress may be an indicator of problems which should be diagnosed and corrected, if possible.

It is also of value to itemize specific strengths and weaknesses for each player so that individual instruction, practice, and coaching can be planned and undertaken.

If a conditioning program is used, it is important to record initial measures of height, weight, strength factors, resting pulse rate, and pulse rate recovery time in interval training. Periodic measurements will indicate not only the rate of progress, but the level of conditioning so that the expected effort under stress and fatigue rate may be anticipated.

Team Information. The team's functioning on offense and defense must be constantly evaluated. Questions which may be considered include: (1) What do we do best? Why? How can we capitalize on it? (2) What do we do well that can be improved? How? (3) What do we do least effectively? Why? How can this be minimized as a vulnerability? What measures are possible to improve? (4) How do factors of personnel use affect the system? Are certain players more or less effective when used in certain combinations, when given certain responsibilities? (5) Does each player know what is expected of her? Does she know how she can best contribute to the team effort? (6) How does the use of a given system of offense affect the ability to play defense? Was bad passing a reason for bad sets? Was the bad passing due to our coverage behind the block? (7) Are players being used to their greatest advantage to the team? Is the outstanding player underworked; overworked? These are some examples of the constant assessments that are required.

Prerequisites. Any method of evaluation used must be valid: that is, it must measure what it proposes, or the data gathered will be deceiving and false. Information gathered should be objective and free from the bias of the recorder. If judgments are to be made, the person judging should have as many guidelines as possible to follow. The procedure should be able to be consistently applied. Variables which would affect performance should be kept to a minimum. To be effective the evaluation procedures should be systematic and functional.

Much time and effort can be spent in attempting to secure measurements and statistics. This time is well worth it if the information can be easily recorded and processed, and if it will give the coach greater insights into individual or team performance. If the results give an incorrect picture of the situation, are easily misinterpreted, or give no more information than the coach would gain by mere observation, the time is totally wasted.

Interdependence of Performance Factors in Volleyball. It is difficult to gather pure statistical information in volleyball. The success of the spiker is dependent upon the success of the setter. The setter must receive a good pass to be able to set. Often line-up position or position in relation to an opponent will affect team members inequitably if numbers of successful attempts or percentages of successful plays are calculated.

Intangibles of Performance. There are some factors of performance which cannot be measured. It is not possible to measure the impact of a team leader upon the other players' performance during a match. Poise, confidence, spirit, desire, and experience are all factors which have been known to enhance the probability of success. The coach should be realistic about assessing these factors, keeping perspective, but never minimizing their overall effect when determining line-up or considering game situation alternatives.

Broad Approach to Evaluation There is no best method of measuring team or individual performance. There are a number of techniques for gathering information which may be helpful to the coach. Each technique may have a specific value, but may also have limitations. It is the function of the coach to select the combination of techniques which gather the most information as efficiently as possible. It is of primary importance to keep in mind the limitations of any particular technique. It may be that some information is useless by itself and can only be helpful when weighed in the light of other factors. The information gathered can only be used to supplement the human, emotional, and physical factors which must be considered in making judgments.

Coach's Bias. Final decisions as to line-up, use of offense and defense, or practice demands should be made in as enlightened a fashion as possible. The coach must make every effort to gather information which is valid and reliable to assist in making judgments. Beyond this, however, when evidence in favor of or against a given method conflicts, an arbitrary decision must be made. When making these kinds of decisions it is important that the coach's personal bias not be a factor.

Also, when making assessments of player ability it is important to allow room for changes in judgments. One practice or one match may not be indicative of what a player can do. Assessments should be made on an accumulation of data about the player. The fair coach will give the player a chance to try and try again, and will work with the player to solve individual problems in performance.

Evaluation with the Players. For evaluation to have its full value, the results of evaluation should be shared with the players and team. This is essential for progress and motivation. Systematic procedures should be established so that this occurs on a regular basis, for both team and individuals.

Incidence Charts. When a record is made of the number of times a given thing occurred, it is best done on an incidence chart. There have been a number of attempts to develop these for volleyball. Most are limited in value unless a total picture of performance can be recorded. For example, it may be possible to tally the number of successful spikes made and figure a percentage with the number of attempts. Since the spiker is dependent on the setter for a good set, her performance can only be considered in relation to the quality of the set. A recording scheme can be developed to indicate the degree of success on the spike keyed with the quality of the set for a more complete picture.

Assessing the quality of a set or the degree of success of a spike places the recorder in a position of having to make these judgments. Criteria must be established to insure that the judgments are consistent or no two matches or practice sessions will be evaluated in the same manner.

Another weakness of the incidence chart, especially when so many factors must be recorded, is that the final ratios are skewed if the recorder misses a single incident. For example, if a spiker attempts 5 spikes and is highly successful with 3, and the recorder misses seeing one successful spike, the incidence chart ratio would show a fifty percent efficiency, rather than the actual sixty percent efficiency. Missing an incident on occasion is highly likely when the recorder is looking down to the recording sheet.

Techniques of Evaluating Performance

In order that incidence charts be used to greatest value, it is important to remember: (1) the recorder must be trained and knowledgeable; (2) avoid incidence records which require a qualitative judgment; (3) if a judgment is necessary, criteria must be established to guide the consistency of the judgment; (4) if several factors are being tallied, a spotter is essential to call the incidents, in which case the spotter must be trained to make quality judgments.

Some factors in volleyball lend themselves more to the incidence technique than the illustration given above. These are more quantitative in nature and include: (1) number of service aces; (2) number of serves forcing a pass to remain in the backcourt; (3) areas of the floor where successful spikes fall; (4) number of balls blocked which rebound back for immediate winning of point, and many others of a similar quantitative nature.

Diagnostic Charts. These charts would be in the form of a checklist of either positive or negative factors in technique execution or offensive and defensive. The coach watches the player or team and checks the appropriate space to indicate the observed action. For example, a positive checklist for the forearm pass might be done as follows:

	Always	Usually	Never
Stance—Uses forward stride	——	——	——
Flexes leg in ready position	——	——	——
Arms—Has a flat rebound surface	——	——	——
Keeps arm out from body	——	——	——
Produces accurate rebound angle	——	——	——
Producing force—Uses legs for force	——	——	——
Restricts arm swing	——	——	——

A negative chart might have value in that it identifies the specific error. In either case, this diagnostic chart is useful in that specific factors are recorded which can be referred to for establishing practice and coaching at a later time.

It is often difficult, however, to construct satisfactory checklists. The problems lie in avoiding ambiguities in the wording and establishing an efficient checking process.

Visual Recordings. Several methods of preparing a visual reproduction are now available to the volleyball coach for use to aid the player or team in improving performance. These include: (1) The graph-check camera which photographs eight sequences on Polaroid film for immediate viewing. The basic techniques of individual performance can be viewed by the player and her strengths and weaknesses can be clearly identified. (2) 8mm or 16mm films of individual or team performance are most helpful. The processing takes some time so that the immediate evaluation of performance is not possible.

(3) Television tape recordings are ideal. Immediate play-back equipment is usually a part of the system and so affords analysis and coaching following performance, if desired.

To use any of these methods, planning must be done to insure maximum value. These planning factors include: (1) the filming, taping, and processing should be done by a knowledgeable technician; (2) the angles of viewing desired should be planned; (3) a viewing time should be planned for coaches to evaluate, (4) unless working with individual performers where immediate review can be done, the team viewing time and space should be carefully planned; (5) the coach should develop a systematic procedure for viewing to get the maximum value for the time spent; (6) develop a scheme for written evaluations to be used as a basis for further practice or game plans.

Part Five

Physical Training Principles

13

Training, Conditioning, and Prevention of Injury

During the course of a volleyball match, the player's body is placed under constant stress. Upon demand, the body must be prepared to move with agility, speed, and power, often over extended periods of time. In order that it will respond at will, a high level of conditioning is required. The major factors involved in conditioning are strength, speed, flexibility, and endurance. Conditioning, coupled with the development of skill in performance, will provide the maximum opportunity for a woman to reach her potential as an athlete. As the level of conditioning is increased, the potential for accident and injury decreases.

The entire volleyball program should be carried on in an environment that will insure the player the maximum amount of safety. Before presenting some specific suggestions about the various aspects of conditioning, some ideas regarding health practices and the prevention of injuries are given.

Prior to the beginning of each season each player should be examined by a physician to insure that she is physically able to participate in the vigorous activity that will be demanded. The examination should be thorough and include an analysis of the function of all the systems of the body which will undergo stress in conditioning, practice, and play. Special attention should be given to an evaluation of old injuries and their vulnerability to recurrence. The coach should receive a verification of each player's clearance. If a restriction is placed upon any player, a detailed description of its nature and extent should be received.

Numerous hazards to safety can be presented in competitive volleyball. To prevent the possibility of injury as a result of carelessness, the following are suggested:

1. Knee pads are mandatory for all players. Pads should be properly fitted to allow maximum circulation. Pads should be worn at the ankles when not in use during practice or matches.
2. Floor surfaces should be properly maintained for cleanliness and to provide a good surface for traction.
3. Standards should be placed at least three feet from the court sidelines. Cranks of ratchets should be collapsible or covered with padding to prevent injury, should a player fall into the standard. Standard bases should be as flat as possible. Support cables should be placed to present the least hazard to a player moving off court for a recovery. A "V" or "Y" cable is often installed to provide maximum support for the standard. These cables are extremely hazardous and should be padded and draped with flags or towels so that the players can more easily see them while moving.
4. All courts should have maximum space available around them. Projections such as corners of bleachers and open doors, or loose equipment such as tables, chairs, and extra standards should be kept clear of the near-court area.
5. During practice and game warm-up loose balls near the movement of players are hazardous. All players should be required to look out for all other players (including opponents) by properly storing balls not in use, and by immediately warning a player who might be in danger of a ball under foot.
6. Proper equipment is essential. Quality leather balls should be used. Inflation of the balls should be made at the same air pressure and temperature in which the ball will be used. Increased altitude or temperature will cause the internal pressure of the ball to increase.
7. Proper clothing is essential. Shoes should have a good traction sole and be well fitted to prevent blisters. There should be no foot movement inside the shoe. Extra socks can prevent this. It is recommended that a wool sock be worn next to the skin because of its softness and absorbent qualities when moist. Cotton socks tend to harden, and the fibers create friction with the foot when saturated with moisture.

Clothing should allow for freedom of movement. Long-sleeve shirts may be worn to prevent floor burns on the arms on recovery plays and to somewhat protect the arms from the repeated pounding of the ball when fielding hard-hit spikes and serves.

8. It is imperative that all injuries or ill health, even the most minor, be reported to the coach immediately. What may appear to be minor may become serious if stressed.

Appropriate Progressions and Warm-up

The coach must carefully analyze the physical demands placed upon the players at each phase of conditioning and practice, and provide for appropriate warm-up for it. It is also necessary to adhere to proper progressions and accurate executions for some phases of skill development to prevent injury. For instance, prior to work on the shoulder roll the player should: (1) have appropriate back, neck, and shoulder flexibility; (2) learn the basic technique on mats; and (3) be admonished to do the lunge prior to the roll from a position already close to the floor.

Health Practices

Players should be encouraged to take excellent care of their health. It is recommended that players (1) maintain sound nutritional practices with three balanced meals daily; (2) get at least eight hours of sleep each night; (3) avoid the use of alcohol and tobacco; (4) use medication and drugs only on physician's recommendation and prescription, and notify the coach immediately if this occurs.

It is important that practice and game clothing be laundered after each use. This is essential to limit the possibility of infections and irritations of the skin.

Showers with soap and hot water should be taken immediately following each practice and match.

The feet require special care. In addition to fitting shoes properly, care should be taken to dry the feet thoroughly to prevent the development of fungus infections. Toenails should be trimmed and callouses kept soft by using lotions. Any foot problems should be immediately referred to a physician.

Injuries

Injuries will occur during practice and matches. The coach should be competent in handling the emergency situation for all injuries. The reader is referred to the training book reference in the bibliography (2) as an excellent source for basic procedures. The coach can care for the minor injuries with basic first-aid techniques, but if there is any question regarding the seriousness of an injury, the player should be referred to a physician. After serious injury or illness a clearance from the physician should be required before participation is resumed. After injury a referral to a therapist or trainer is highly desirable to facilitate the rehabilitation process. The coach should be aware that after illness or injury the player will require a period of retraining to be able to respond adequately to practice and match demands.

The player who has an old injury to a joint, or one who has recently recovered from such an injury, may need to protect the area by supportive taping for both practice and competition. This should be done faithfully to preclude further injury until the time when the surrounding muscles, tendons, and ligaments are sufficiently strengthened to support the joint. Fingers, thumbs, ankles and knees are especially vulnerable to the recurrence of injury. *Protective Taping*

The basic factors to be developed in a conditioning program are: (1) strength—the ability to exert force against a resistance; (2) speed—the ability to move the body through space at a given rate; (3) flexibility—the ability to move body parts through the fullest range possible; and (4) endurance—the ability of the bodily systems to adapt and function efficiently in a sustained manner during prolonged activity. Conditioning

There is an interrelationship between some of these factors. When working for increases in strength, muscular endurance will occur. Since speed is a combination of ability to apply force and to do it quickly, increases in strength will result in increases in speed. To improve endurance one must work the body for extended periods of time. As this is done some gains in strength are made in the body parts that function. (1)

Gains in strength, speed, flexibility, and endurance are all accomplished through the application of overload during training. To overload is to cause the body to work harder than it is accustomed. Overloading in a conditioning program can be done by increasing (1) workload, (2) repetitions, (3) speed, and (4) duration for the activity that is being performed. *Overload Principle*

Strength is important for the volleyball player to be able to jump well and spike the ball with power. The development of strength depends upon the following factors. (1,2) *Strength*

1. Overload is imposed by working against a resistance which is almost the maximum that the player can move for ten repetitions. Progressive increases in the amount of resistance or the speed of repetitions will produce increases in overload.
2. A program should be composed of 2–3 sets of work of 4 to 10 repetitions each.
3. All resistance exercises should be done through a full range of motion.
4. For maximum strength development the resistance should be met at the specific angle at which power is needed in performing the technique in the sport.
5. Gains in strength will be rapid in early stages, but will decrease as the player approaches potential. For maximum results, at least 3 workouts a week are required.
6. Gains in strength can be maintained by one full contraction against maximum resistance per week.

Table 13.1 illustrates the strength demands for a volleyball player and suggests some exercises for strength development. Suggestions for conducting the weight training program are presented later in this chapter.

Speed Speed of movement is important to the volleyball player on both offense and defense. A major factor in the development of speed is the increase in strength of the muscles that execute the action. It is also highly desirable to improve flexibility so that body parts can move freely through a full range of motion. The speed of muscle contraction is individual from one muscle group to another and from player to player. To insure maximum opportunity for increasing speed, the techniques to be performed should be executed with all the forces applied to the action moving as directly to that purpose as possible, (1). For example, to increase running speed the feet should point straight ahead and the arms and legs should move with as little lateral action as possible. The body also should move with the center of gravity staying on a line that is parallel to the floor.

Flexibility Flexibility is very important to the volleyball player. With the ability to move each body part through a full range of motion the player will more readily be able to improve skill. Flexibility also aids in the prevention of injuries, (2). There are two methods of increasing flexibility, or stretching the muscles, tendons, and ligaments that surround the joints: (1) ballistic stretch—bobbing or bouncing; and (2) static stretch—a slow sustained stretch, holding position at the extent of stretch. De Vries (1) has done research in this area and has found that both methods are equally effective in improving flexibility, but the static stretch causes little muscle soreness which frequently accompanies the ballistic stretch. Table 13.2 presents some exercises for flexibility for areas of the body that are important to the volleyball player. The overload principle is applied by progressively stretching the area further each time the exercise is done or by stretching, holding, and then stretching further.

Endurance Two forms of endurance are of concern to the volleyball player: (1) muscular endurance—or the ability of muscle groups to sustain effort or frequent contractions for a period of time; and (2) cardio-respiratory endurance—the ability of the total body to sustain an activity for prolonged periods.

Muscular endurance is greatly increased with gains in strength. Work with light resistance and overloading by increasing the speed and repetition of contractions will develop muscular endurance, (1,2). The volleyball player must develop endurance of the muscles of the legs for jumping and the shoulder and upper trunk muscles for spiking and blocking.

The following factors are important to development of cardio-respiratory endurance:

1. The major objectives of a training program are to increase the ability of the circulatory system to transport oxygen and to carry an oxygen debt. (1)

Table 13.1 Strength Development for Volleyball

Volleyball Technique and Action	Muscle Group	Suggested Exercise
1. Jumping and Leg Endurance for Movement	1. a. Plantar flexorsgastrocnemius and soleus	1. a. Toe raising with weights in hands; start with toes on board 2 inches high to gain the flexion used in the jump.
	b. Knee extensors and hip extensors	b. Half squats with weights in hands held at shoulder height; start at knee flexion at which jump is started.
2. Spiking a. Trunk action—backswing	2. a. Erector spinae	2. a. Lie on end of bench, face down, with feet held down, end of bench just below waist. Place hands behind head. Raise head and shoulders as high as possible by arching the back. To increase work, hold small weights (1–5 lb.) in hands.
b. Trunk action—hitting the ball	b. Abdominals	b. With knees bent and feet held down, lie on back. Curl the trunk upward to a sitting position. To increase work, place hands behind head; or do on incline board with feet higher than head; or do with small weights in hands held at shoulder height.
c. Arm action—armswing for jump	c. Latissimus Dorsi, Deltoid, Rhomboids, Trapezius, Teres Major, Pectorals, Biceps Brachii	c. Stand with weights in each hand; bend forward at waist so upper trunk is parallel to floor. Swing arms backward and forward at moderate speed, being sure to keep arms fully extended, moving through full range of motion.
d. Hitting action—shoulder	d. Pectorals	d. Sit with elbow raised as high as possible, hand behind head, shoulder rotated back so that elevated elbow is in line with the line of the shoulders. Partner places resistance to inside of elbow. Bring elbow through resistance toward midline of the body. Keep elbow elevated throughout both arms.
e. Hitting action—arm	e. Elbow extensors, wrist flexors	e. Sit with elbow raised as high as possible, elbow pointing up and forward, hand cocked behind head. Holding weight in hand, extend elbow. To keep elbow from lowering until arm is extended, place other hand under arm near the shoulder. Both arms.
3. Ball Handling a. Wrist action	3. a. Wrist flexors, wrist extensors	3. a. Attach a weight to the end of a rope, attaching the other end to a 15″ piece of dowling. Repeatedly, roll the weighted rope up and down by curling the wrists. Hold at chest level, with elbows slightly bent.
b. Finger action	b. finger flexors	b. Repeatedly, squeeze a small rubber or sponge ball in each hand.

Table 13.2 Improving Flexibility for Volleyball (Static Stretch)

Body Area	Suggested Exercise
1. Low Back, Back of Hip and Thigh	1. Stand with left foot crossed in front of right, place left hand on right shoulder. Bend forward reaching left elbow to left knee. Do to each side.
2. Low Back	2. Sit with soles of feet together and knees out to side. Try to reach head down as close to feet as possible.
3. Upper Back	3. Lie on back. Raise feet and curl up so that feet touch floor above the head.
4. Upper trunk Twist	4. Sit with legs crossed in a tailor's position. Reach to grasp left thigh with both hands. Turn trunk to left and look as far back to left as possible. Do to each side.
5. Shoulder Stretch	5. Bring right hand over shoulder to back. Bring left hand under shoulder to back. Hook fingers and hold. Repeat to other side.
6. Low Trunk	6. Lie on abdomen. Reach down and grasp ankles as legs are flexed at knee. Hold head up.
7. Gastrocnemius Stretch	7. Stand 3 to 4 feet from wall. Keeping heels on floor and back straight, rest palm of hands on the wall.

2. One of the simplest methods of measuring the effect of training is to chart progressive decreases in the resting pulse rate. (2)
3. Endurance is gained by using total body activity and overloading with either amount of workload, the frequency of the work or the duration of the work time. (1,2)
4. Interval training is highly recommended as a method of increasing endurance, (1,2). This will be described in a later section.
5. The progress of training can be negatively affected by working to exhaustion. (1)

The volleyball player can increase cardio-respiratory endurance by a number of methods, including jogging, running, rope skipping, bicycling, or stair running. The training program should be individually charted. Each player should be encouraged to work hard and push herself beyond her previous efforts.

Endurance can be developed while working on speed, quick reaction, and proper body mechanics for movement. Intensive work periods emphasizing sliding, starting, stopping, changing direction, and jumping will be effective in enhancing endurance if the overload principle is applied. These activities could be incorporated into a type of interval training program, provided the elements of an interval training program are adhered to.

Weight training is the most advantageous method of developing strength through progressively increasing overload. Some girls and women hesitate to engage in weight training for fear of getting "bulging" muscles or appearing masculine. This is basically a misconception. It is observed by Klafs and Arnheim (2) that although muscle fibers do increase in size with strength development, strength can be developed to an increase of about three times without a proportional increase in muscle bulk. If weight training is a part of a total conditioning program, usually the muscle fiber increase replaces losses of fatty tissue. The result is an improved appearance through the contouring of the body part. It is the observation of the authors that girls who have feminine appearance and mannerisms when beginning a weight program will lose neither of these qualities while engaged in it.

Some suggestions for safe conduct of a weight-training program for volleyball include:

1. Study the strength development requirements for each technique carefully. Select a simple sequence of exercises which will work the desired areas. There are many exercises for each area so select one good one.
2. Know the exercise fully before presenting it. Present the posture, the work sequence, weight selection, speed, repetitions, and safety problems.
3. Test each player for her maximum weight for one effort. Eighty percent of that will approximate what she can do for ten repetitions. If, after a number of repetitions, this is too heavy, reduce the weight appropriately.
4. Increments in weights for most girls should be one to five pounds for arm and shoulder exercises. Ten pound increments can be used for the stronger leg muscle groups.
5. Progress charts on which to record date, exercises, weight repetitions, or duration should be kept for each girl.
6. It is imperative that the weight-training area be properly supervised at all times. Players should not be allowed to experiment with weights or exercises in which they have not been instructed.

Various types of weights are available commercially. They include dumbbells, barbells, cuffs, boots, and weight machines. Weights can also be improvised by filling small bags with varying amounts of sand or by doing the same to various sizes of plastic jugs (with handles) in which household cleaners are often sold. Most exercises, described in this chapter and in the references for this chapter, are adaptable to the various types of weights.

Interval training has been widely used in track to bring runners nearer to their potential. The method is simple, involving the execution of a bout of work (running) at a given pace for a given distance, followed by a recovery period in which the runner jogs until reaching a given level of recovery. The work and recovery periods are repeated any number of times. The overload is applied by increasing the number of work bouts while keeping pace and distance

Types of Conditioning Programs

Weight Training

Interval Training

constant. De Vries (1) suggests that work periods of thirty seconds are best, with rest periods long enough for the pulse rate to return to 120 beats per minute. Klafs and Arnheim (2) suggest that the pulse should return to 80 to 90 percent of normal during the rest period.

Circuit Training This system of training allows work on resistance exercises and other conditioning exercises in sequence. The object is to do a sequence of exercises by moving from station to station around the work area. The player attempts to do a given amount of work within a target time, moving on to the next station as soon as the work is completed. Overload for the circuit is done by either increasing the work to be done within a given time, by doing the same amount of work in less time, or by doing as much work as possible in increased amounts of time. Circuit training works for large groups and is extremely motivational and efficient in terms of time used.

Off Season Conditioning For the athlete to reach the maximum level of conditioning for a season, it is beneficial to approach the preseasonal training phase in good fitness. A high degree of conditioning can be maintained off season by participating in other sports or by maintaining an active program of running and exercises. The physical demands of off-season work are usually much less for the athlete than those in season. After the season she should be encouraged to decrease her caloric intake to avoid the increase in body fat which can occur as she decreases her activity level.

Warm-Up There are two purposes of warm-up: (1) rehearsal of the activity to be performed and (2) increase muscle and blood temperature. De Vries (1) has summarized the research regarding warm-up and suggests that:

1. Warm-up of the whole body, in terms of muscle and blood temperature, can improve performance.
2. Warm-up is important to avoid muscle soreness and injury.
3. Warm-up must be suited to the individual and the athletic activity.
4. The warm-up should be done hard enough and long enough to raise the internal temperature. Perspiring is usually an indication of this increase in temperature.
5. The raise in muscle temperature usually persists from 45 to 80 minutes. This suggests that substitutes who have adequately warmed up prior to the match may be called upon for maximum exertion with little danger of injury.
6. Warm-up activities which will provide a practice for the game are preferred.

Conditioning takes hard work and causes some pain to be endured. If the potential for performance is to be reached, the volleyball player must work to improve her conditioning. The coach is responsible to structure the most positive environment possible. The coach can work with the players, encourage them, measuring and charting improvement. Music during exercises makes time go quickly. When exercises are performed in stationary positions, such as on weight machines or bicycle ergometers, films may be shown to alleviate boredom. If the intensity of the program is consistent with the objective of the players for developing ability to play volleyball, few problems should be encountered.

Mental Attitude Toward Conditioning

1. De Vries, Herbert A. *Physiology of Exercises for Physical Education and Athletics. Dubuque, Iowa:* Wm. C. Brown Company Publishers, 1982.
2. Klafs, Carl E., and Arnheim, Daniel D. *Modern Principles of Athletic Training.* St. Louis: The C. V. Mosby Company, 1977.

Bibliography

Glossary

attack n. The offense; v. to hit the ball into the opponent's court.

attack block A blocking technique designed to intercept the flight of the ball before it crosses the net.

auxiliary setter A front-row player in the multiple offense who is assigned to set the ball when the setter from the back row makes the first contact of the ball on that side.

back set A set executed over the head, behind the setter.

block A defensive technique by one or more players who attempt to intercept the ball near the net.

cover An offensive positioning taken as the hitter attacks the ball to field any ball rebounding from the block.

defense The skills and strategies employed by a team when the ball is controlled by the opponents.

dig A defensive skill used to recover the opponent's attack by cushioning the ball on the forearms.

dink An offensive technique in which a potential spiker contacts the ball on her fingers with only slight forward motion of the arm, sending the ball over or around the block and into the opponent's court.

dive A defensive technique used to recover a ball by extending to prone position to contact the ball and recovering on the floor.

double hit Consecutive contacts of the ball by one player; usually the result of uneven contact which is illegal.

forearm pass A ball played off the forearms in an underhand manner.

free ball A ball passed over the net to the opponents which travels in an upward trajectory.

hitter A spiker.

middle-back defense A team defensive formation that uses the middle-back player to dig deep spikes

middle-up defense A team defensive formation that uses the middle-back player to dig short dink shots.

motor learning An internal change within an individual which is inferred from a relatively permanent change in performance which results from practice.

multiple offense A three hitter offense in which the ball is set by a back-row player.

net recovery An attempt to play a ball that has been hit into the net.

no block defense Defensive positions assumed when opponents cannot agressively spike the ball.

offense The skills and strategies employed by a team controlling the ball.

off-hand spike A spike executed from a set approaching the spiker from the side of her nonspiking hand.

off-speed spike A ball hit from the normal spiking position with reduced speed of arm swing.

on-hand spike A spike executed from a set approaching the spiker from the same side as the spiker's hitting hand.

overhand pass A technique executed with both hands that is used to project the ball in the same direction that the passer is facing.

overset A set ball which passes over the net into the opponent's court, potentially available to be spiked by an opponent.

pass-set-spike play The basic offensive pattern; three contacts of the ball consisting of a receiving pass, and a set-up pass to a third player who attacks the ball above net height into the opponent's court.

play sets Predetermined set variations called by the setter or hitter.

roll A defensive technique used to recover a ball by extending the body laterally or forward to the floor and rolling over to quickly return to an upright position.

save A recovery of a ball which would have hit the court except for an extreme effort of the player moving well beyond her normal range of coverage.

serve An offensive technique used to put the ball in play by contacting it with the hand.

service ace A service that lands in the opponent's court for a point without being touched.

set The technique used to place the ball in a position for a player to attack.

soft block A blocking technique in which the forearms are held parallel to the net while the hands are parallel to the net or tilted slightly backwards.

spike A hard hit into the opponent's court.

switch An intentional, strategic interchange of positions on the court.

technique player A player of all-around ability frequently brought into the net from the back-court for setting purposes.

References

Beutedstahl, Dieter, *Volleyball: Playing to Win.* New York: Arco, 1978
Bertucci, Robert, ed. *Championship Volleyball by Experts,* 2nd ed. Highland Falls,
    N.Y.: Leisure Press, 1982

Johnson, M. L. and Johnson, DeWayne J. *Volleyball.* Fairfield, N.J.: American
    Press 1981

Keller, Val. *Point, Game and Match.* Hollywood, California: Creative Sports Books,
    1968.

MacGregor, Barrie, *Volleyball.* E. P. Publishing England, Sterling, 1982

Scates, Allen E. *Winning Volleyball.* Boston: Allyn and Bacon, Inc., 1984.
Scates, Allen E., and Ward, Jane. *Volleyball.* Allyn and Bacon, Inc., 1975.
Schakel, David Jr., *Volleyball.* Fairfield, N.J.: American Press, 1980.

Index

wcb
Wm. C. Brown Publishers
Dubuque, Iowa

ISBN 0-697-07193-6